What people ~~are saying about~~
Becoming a More Thoughtful Leader

You are worth the investment. This book will help you realize the amazing gains in that investment with stories that will touch your heart, and tools that will change your life. Enjoy the read; embrace the possibilities!

—**Chester Elton**, Bestselling Author
of *The Carrot Principle* and *Leading With Gratitude*

When I prepare to read a book by Randy Hain, I always know what I am about to digest: warm wisdom. Randy provides practical, helpful, and relevant counsel in a personal, kind, and friendly manner. This book is nothing less than that. Every chapter solves a problem or furnishes sound advice for your career as a leader. Not only are these words timely for our world today but timeless in their value. Becoming a Thoughtful Leader adds value regardless of your age or context. I recommend this book without any reservation.

—**Tim Elmore**, Bestselling Author, Acclaimed International Speaker, Founder of Growing Leaders and TimElmore.com

Leaders' days are often packed with back-to-back meetings, leaving evenings and weekends to do strategic "work." Sometimes leaders teeter on the edge of burnout, even as they know its costs, and they seek self-development books for all manner of guidance, from making time for personal desires to fulfilling leadership priorities. The genius guidance contained in Randy Hain's newest book, *Becoming a More Thoughtful Leader*, begins with its title. In each chapter's clear and compelling stories, he presents a lesson in "reflection, then action." This work makes a case for simple leadership (and personal) practices for including thoughtfulness in our collective work culture that values brevity and fast decision-making. It's believable and reliable because it's based on Randy's life and work experience. Implement these practices for a higher quality of life for yourself and those you lead.

—**Andrea Chilcote**, Author of *What Leaders Need Now*, Executive Coach and President, Morningstar Ventures Inc.

In *Becoming a More Thoughtful Leader*, Randy Hain illustrates through powerful examples how a look in the mirror and a commitment to continuous growth can be transformative and create a culture where everyone feels valued, motivated, and capable of achieving great success. This book echoes my belief that the best leaders are those who never stop learning and who understand that their growth is intrinsically linked to the growth of their people. *Becoming a More Thoughtful Leader* is a compelling reminder that leadership is not just about being in charge but about taking care of those in your charge. For anyone committed to being a better leader, both for themselves and their team, this book is an essential read!

—**Camye Mackey**, EVP and Chief People, Diversity and Inclusion Officer for the Atlanta Hawks and State Farm Arena

In *Becoming a More Thoughtful Leader*, Randy explores the core traits that distinguish great leaders from good ones, focusing on self-reflection, active listening, empathy, mentoring, and leading by example. The book emphasizes emotional intelligence and relational leadership over traditional methods, urging leaders to prioritize self-awareness and personal growth. Randy stresses the importance of continual self-reflection and honest feedback, showing that true leadership begins within. He also highlights how empathy and active listening help build trust and collaboration, and he offers practical advice for developing these skills. With real-world examples and actionable insights, Randy challenges readers to lead with purpose, integrity, and responsibility. This book serves as an invaluable guide for leaders seeking to make a lasting impact on their teams and organizations.

—**Juan Perez**, Chief Information Officer for Salesforce

I know of no more thoughtful leader and friend than Randy Hain. He lives and breathes thoughtfulness, so to have him provide an in-depth look into the topic of what a thoughtful leader displays is a gift. Let's soak up his leadership principles like a sponge; this book is extremely important for today's business times. I am so grateful for you, Randy, not only your wisdom but your humility, consistency, and integrity as a trusted leader.

—**Glen Jackson**, Co-founder, Jackson Spalding

This book is full of uncommonly detailed advice for anyone aspiring to be a great leader. The power of daily reflection leading to continual improvements in self-management and hence remarkably positive impacts on others—both in work and at home—is very compelling. Randy's habits—thoughtfully built over thirty-plus years—can be adopted by any reader. I am in my "fourth quarter" and found this book remarkably stimulating; it was difficult to put down! In sharing his learnings on leadership, Randy Hain, along with the likes of Lencioni, Goleman, and Covey, is a core member of the pantheon of writers on leadership. I plan to recommend and gift this marvelous compendium to clients, friends, and family.

—**Anthony Lynch**, Leadership Coach and Founder of Thoughtful Partners

This book grabbed me from the start and convicted me of my own habits and leadership styles across my career in the corporate world and as a business owner. Randy Hain delivers another compelling anthology packed with sage wisdom, leadership gold, and refreshing authenticity throughout the pages. Whether the reader is a new leader or an experienced leader, these concepts are truly applicable and relevant. I loved how this was organized with a "Think, Do, Think, Do" framework using thoughtful questions at the end of each chapter. Brilliant! I also learned some new concepts, like the power of anointed credibility and the charge of *Ti voglio bene* to use with my clients and mentees. I am grateful to have this

in my personal library and highly recommend it for all leaders and professionals—no matter what stage of career!
—**Ash Merchant**, CEO and Founder, Lionheart Partners

Randy's content is always dead on. And thinking with the reader in mind, I love how Randy structures each chapter with a main point, a few practical and easy to digest examples, and simple reflection questions that seamlessly allow the reader to put into practice.
—**Rick Packer**, CEO, Packer Consulting Group

Randy Hain has taught me to be a more thoughtful leader through his coaching, actions, and advice, and now through *Becoming a More Thoughtful Leader*, anyone can have the privilege of learning from him as well. This book is meant for anyone aspiring to enhance their leadership skills, both professionally and personally. Drawing from his own experiences, Randy Hain offers candid, authentic, and wise insights that readers have come to love from his work. This book stands out for its genuine and raw approach, providing readers with actionable advice and heartfelt guidance. Each chapter is thoughtfully designed with reflection questions, which encourage deep, meaningful conversations, helping readers not only become better leaders in their work but also more thoughtful leaders in life. Everyone will find something in this book that strongly resonates, making it a valuable resource for leaders at every stage of their journey.
—**Kate McCombs**, PhD, Assistant Professor of Management, Entrepreneurship, Management, and Marketing for Samford University

Becoming a More Thoughtful Leader is not just a book for reading; it's a book for doing. Randy Hain has written a refreshing and impactful guide that stands apart from many other leadership books because it is a reflection of his profound journey. It intertwines personal stories and professional experience to guide readers through the nuances of leadership, making it feel like an intimate conversation with a trusted mentor. Having known Randy for almost twenty years, I can confidently say that this book is a true representation of the thoughtfulness and care he has consistently shown in his work with global business leaders. But it's not stuffy; it's personal. It's easy to pick up, read a chapter, and then reflect on the content's meaning both personally and professionally. Like his counsel, it is a call to action for leaders to invest in themselves and those around them.

—**Lisa Bigazzi Tilt**, CEO of Full Tilt Consulting

Randy has a unique talent to give the reader what they need to hear. *Becoming a More Thoughtful Leader* is the playbook for anyone who is in a career reimagination phase of their life. The best practices shared here are not always talked about in career growth and development, but they need to be critical parts of the conversation.

—**Ben Milsom**, Author of *The Fearless Diabetic* and Chief Revenue Officer for Intersport

Becoming a More Thoughtful Leader offers a deeply practical guide for leaders who want to move beyond transactional leadership and develop a more people-centric, thoughtful approach. Randy draws from his wealth of experience as an HR executive and coach, interlacing together personal anecdotes and real-world scenarios that leaders from any industry can relate to. Whether you're a seasoned leader or just starting out in your leadership journey, *Becoming a More Thoughtful Leader* is filled with strategies that will help you cultivate a leadership style that is not only effective but also deeply human.

—**Willie Mazyck,** Global Head of Talent Development, Danaher

Becoming a More Thoughtful Leader is not just a book about being a better leader. It's a book about being a better human being and how to think about life, business, and bringing value to our relationships, community, and the world. I have been using Randy's books and the consolidation of his life experiences to coach those who are coming along after me. I wish I had this resource available to me when I was starting out. The advice from *Becoming a More Thoughtful Leader* is timeless! I will be sharing this thoughtful book with those men and women I am coaching and mentoring well into the future. Thanks again, Randy!

—**Ray V. Padrón**, Retired CEO,
Brightworth Private Wealth

In his new book, Randy Hain has given us characteristically practical guidance and insights that feel both timeless and contemporary. Read this book to learn, grow, and increase your ability to lift up those around you!

—**Louis Gump**, President of Cambian Solutions and Author of
The Inside Innovator: A Practical Guide to Intrapreneurship

Becoming a More Thoughtful Leader is more than just a guide; it's a conversation starter and a catalyst for meaningful change. Whether you're looking to enhance your leadership skills or seeking new ways to engage with your team, this book offers valuable insights and practical advice that can make a real difference in your professional journey. I have known Randy a long time, and he continues to deliver thoughtful, helpful, and practical books for senior leaders.

—**Ira Genser**, CFO for Iconex

This book is an essential guide for leaders at any point in their career. Filled with practical insights and actionable strategies, Randy invites readers to reflect deeply on their personal and professional growth. By encouraging a more thoughtful approach to leadership, *Becoming a More Thoughtful Leader* inspires us to elevate both ourselves and those we lead, fostering a culture of continuous improvement and mutual support.

—**Virginia Means**, Chief People Officer of
United Distributors, Inc.

Randy Hain has guided so many of us toward having a mindset of a greater good and the belief that we can all do well by doing good. In these pages we have a gift from Randy. He takes us to a place where we can reflect through his lens and connect to his decades of experience listening and guiding people. More importantly, we are challenged by Randy to look deeper into ourselves and ask how we can inspire others. All in Randy's approachable, modest writing style that gives us the sense we are sitting with him as we read his books and sharing a cup of coffee. And that is the beauty of this book. Randy is doing good by us in these pages. By the end, Randy lights the path to becoming a more thoughtful leader, but most importantly, we are left with the clarity that a mindset of a greater good will fill our personal cup with achievement and success that cannot be matched.

—**Nathan Hepple**, Founder, HBA Legal
and Big 5 Investments Company Director

Of the many books Randy Hain has written, *Becoming a More Thoughtful Leader* is my favorite thus far. It's the blueprint to the purposeful way in which Randy lives and leads. Each chapter is a treasure trove of knowledge thirty years in the making and, if considered and applied, can catapult leaders both young and seasoned to the next level, bypassing many of the same challenges others have faced along the way. Investing in oneself is often pushed to the back burner of our overfilled calendars, but this is a costly mistake. Within these pages, Randy not only shares how to regain control of your time but clearly explains the far-reaching benefits of doing so. Commit to reading one chapter of *Becoming a More Thoughtful Leader* each day and you'll store up a gratitude surplus that will not only grow you personally but will positively impact those around you. And that is certainly something we can all use.

—**Whitney Teal Mendoza**, Founder, The Teal Bridge

I found myself smiling and doing a lot of "head nodding" when reading this book. As leaders, we often forget that the solutions to our leadership challenges are right in front of us; Randy reminds us of these solutions and helps us make them actionable! *Becoming a More Thoughtful Leader* offers a positive, insightful, and practical perspective on leadership. Randy emphasizing the importance of reflection, empathy, and candor that are critical for any successful leader. He provides real-business examples, reflecting on complex situations and systematically translating his thoughtful guidance into practical and actionable advice. The book also serves as an insightful guide that emphasizes the importance of resilience when navigating difficult conversations. It's a valuable resource for both future and experienced leaders who want to cultivate a more thoughtful and reflective approach to their roles. *Becoming a More Thoughtful Leader* is a must-read for anyone looking to enhance their leadership skills and foster a more inclusive, reflective, and accountable organizational culture.

—**Simon Kaiser**, Chief Operating Officer, Americas, ISS World Service A/S

The post-pandemic business environment is dramatically different in ways that can be either beneficial or harmful, depending on how we respond. Short-term goal setting and unstable or unpredictable economic conditions combined with hybrid working environments and the highest employee turnover rates in history make it challenging for us as executives and organizational leaders to balance the pressures of delivering results while growing our teams and ourselves. Through practical, short testimonies, Randy helps us remember the importance of our human interactions and relationships above material outcomes as the long-term impact and legacy of our lives. At the end of our journey, how we allowed others to transform us and how we transformed those around us to fulfill our providential calling in the workplace and beyond is what will enable us to say, "I have competed well; I have finished the race; I have kept the faith" (2 Timothy 4:7).

—**Ricardo Alvarado**, Director, Jabian Consulting

What I like, appreciate, and value in Randy's most recent book is how engaging and pragmatic it is. Many books written by business leaders feel like textbooks you have to work through to get to the end. Randy's writing style is approachable and leaves you with actionable steps at the end of each chapter. His liberal use of personal and professional examples throughout the book means the content feels authentic and relatable, regardless of what stage you are in your career. He is able to connect with people through his writing, creating a shared experience for his readers. His chapter on turning vulnerabilities into something positive resonated with me personally; my own willingness to acknowledge my professional weaknesses and create alliances with colleagues who can help educate and support me in those areas has made all the difference in my ability to impact our business. As expected, Randy has written another book that proves valuable for anyone who takes the time to read it, and incorporate the suggested actions into their daily practices.

—**Jodi Weintraub**, Global Chief People Officer, GroupM Nexus

Randy Hain has done it again. *Becoming a More Thoughtful Leader* is a practical guide to helping leaders at all levels take a step back from the urgency epidemic and truly reflect on how they want to show up to themselves and others. Through probing questions, reflections, personal stories, and practical steps, this book can help any leader implement the proper disciplines in one's life to be the leader that they and others need today more than ever.

—**Brandon Smith**, Founder of The Worksmiths and author of
The Author vs. Editor Dilemma and *The Hot Sauce Principle*

Whether you are the leader of a global organization, a team, or a family, you will find valuable insights in Randy Hain's latest book, *Becoming a More Thoughtful Leader*. Mr. Hain provides wisdom and guidance for all leaders and, more importantly, practical actions you can take to grow in your ability to influence, engage, and ignite your team. I highly recommend this book.

—**John Riordan**, CEO of Harvest Technology Group

I am never disappointed when Randy shares words of advice and practical wisdom. There is always something relevant and timely I can act on that will help me become a better leader and human being. That's what we all strive for, right? In every chapter of *Becoming a More Thoughtful Leader*, Randy provides practical and actionable ideas, gleamed from his experiences, that will challenge and equip you to strive to be a great servant leader through purposeful self-reflection, self-investment, and investment in those with whom you work and serve. I am already implementing several of these newly learned ideas. Leaders of every age and level will want to read and share this book.

—**Mike Bickerstaff**, President, Virtue@Work

Randy Hain's *Becoming a More Thoughtful Leader* is a wonderful compendium of practical wisdom, full of timely reminders for busy people. The vast scope covers an impressive array of topics—including providing feedback, cultivating patience, and becoming a better listener. I was especially moved by his chapter on friendship. These virtues apply equally to the professional and personal realms. Hain distills decades of experience in one highly readable book, and I offer my most robust recommendation!

—**Paul J. Voss**, PhD, President Ethikos and
Associate Professor, Georgia State University

Randy has truly outdone himself with this book! His practical, insightful advice, grounded in real-life experiences, continues to be a guiding light in my personal and professional development. Randy emphasizes the importance of understanding our own biases, convictions, and expectations as key to growth and improvement. I find myself turning to his wisdom whenever I encounter challenges or feel stuck. This book has earned a permanent place in my library, and I can't wait to share its invaluable lessons with those I mentor and coach.

—**Amelia Fox**, Chief Strategy Officer,
Chief of Staff for Lutheran Services Florida

In this insightful work, Randy offers a refreshing perspective on leadership that extends far beyond the boardroom. He encourages us to embrace patience, kindness, and understanding, providing practical strategies to enhance our effectiveness as leaders in the workplace. More importantly, these principles seamlessly translate into our roles as parents and family members, fostering more nurturing home environments. In a world often driven by self-interest and profit margins, Randy's book serves as a calm, reflective voice, challenging us to elevate our leadership approach. His gentle yet powerful words inspire us to strive for better without dwelling on past missteps. As someone who has led sports teams to victory and now shapes future sports business leaders, I find Randy's message both timely and essential. I'm proud to call Randy a friend, and I'm confident that readers will discover a wise, encouraging companion within the pages of this book. Whether you're leading a sports team, a business unit, or a family, *Becoming a More Thoughtful Leader* offers valuable insights to enrich your leadership journey.

—**Darin W. White**, PhD, Hall of Fame College
Soccer Coach/National Championship Winner and
Executive Director, Center for Sports Analytics
at Samford University

Becoming a More Thoughtful Leader has opened my eyes to the power of self-reflection. It encourages me to embrace authenticity and purpose throughout my leadership journey. Randy Hain excels at blending practical advice with profound insights, offering a clear path to becoming a leader who is effective, genuine, and empathetic. This book challenges conventional leadership approaches and presents a refreshing perspective centered on empathy and self-awareness. *Becoming a More Thoughtful Leader* will undoubtedly be a staple alongside Essential Wisdom and Upon Reflection as I continue to lead thoughtfully and make a lasting impact on my peers and those I serve.

—**Misty Brown**, Assistant Commissioner,
Southeastern Conference

Becoming a More
THOUGHTFUL
LEADER

Practical Insights to Spark
Meaningful Growth

Randy Hain

Foreword by Andreas Widmer,
author of *The Art of Principled Entrepreneurship:
Creating Enduring Value*

SERVIAM PRESS

ISBN: 978-1-7377244-7-6   (softcover)
ISBN: 978-1-7377244-8-3   (e-book)

Published by Serviam Press, LLC
www.serviampress.com

*This book is dedicated with great appreciation to
all the thoughtful leaders I respect and admire who are sincerely
committed to learning and growing . . . and helping everyone
around them to thrive.*

CONTENTS

FOREWORD

Pursuing one's potential as a leader is never fully achieved but always a journey of becoming. This is why we must increasingly focus on the path rather than the goal. Don't defer what needs to be done, what's in your heart. Don't wait for "one day" to realize your full potential, to "one day" create that special work culture within your team. Don't wait for that one big action you're preparing for in the future—do it now.

In my experience working with many leaders throughout my career, I've found that what truly differentiates a great, thoughtful leader isn't so much the "what"—what methods we use for innovation, what systems of management, what marketing strategies, or what competitive tactics we implement. What really makes the difference is the "why." At the core of this is your intent for others. Why are you leading?

The late Saint Pope John Paul II often emphasized that it's all about love. I had the privilege of working with him as a Swiss Guard many years ago, and he showed me firsthand what it feels like to be part of the team of a truly thoughtful leader. I avoid saying "worked for" because he insisted that no one ever works "for" anyone; we only ever work "with" one another. Work is something we do not just for the material outcome, but for the transformation it can have on us. When we work well, he'd point out, we don't just make more—we become more.

It is this understanding that distinguishes great leaders. They genuinely love their team members. Unfortunately, in English, there's only one word for love, which can sound a bit strange in the workplace context. But in Italian, the language accommodates distinctions. You wouldn't say, "*Ti amo*" ("I love you") to an employee—that's reserved for familial and romantic love. Instead, you'd say, "*Ti voglio bene*" ("I want your good"). John Paul II highlighted that this is the root of love: wanting the good of the other. When we love someone, we want their good. But then he'd pause and ask, "What 'good' do you want for them?"

I want to stop here and let you answer that for yourself: "What good do I wish for each of my team members?"

John Paul II explained to his team that his thought for us was about our ultimate good, our eternal happiness. He literally wished us to reach heaven. It didn't matter to him if we believed in life after death or even in heaven. It was enough for him to believe it himself and thus to wish on us the highest ideal he could think of for us—even when we "just" worked together.

This ultimate good that the thoughtful leader wishes for their team is crucial for the here-and-now, for the small decisions we make every day, because our immediate actions often have long-term effects. Thoughtful leaders realize for themselves that if I love you as my teammate, customer, investor, or community member, why would I make you do something, give you something, or do something for you that would hinder your eternal happiness and fulfillment?

It's not that thoughtful leaders don't have end goals in mind or that they lack KPIs for employees, customer satisfaction scores, social impact measurements, or exit strategies. It's just that their goals transcend these short-term measurements. The ultimate reward they're pursuing is not just of this world. The exit strategy of great leaders is happiness and eternity. That's why the path is intrinsic to the goal. The path is work, and the goal is wholesomeness, human excellence, and holiness.

Leadership is a journey that constantly challenges us to grow, reflect, and adapt. In a world where the pace of business often demands immediate results, Randy Hain offers a much-needed pause—a space for leaders to become more thoughtful, deliberate, and impactful. *Becoming a More Thoughtful Leader* is not just a book of advice; it's a roadmap to intentional leadership that transcends the workplace and permeates every aspect of our lives.

Randy's insights, drawn from decades of experience and countless coaching conversations, resonate with the wisdom that true leadership begins with self-awareness and the sincere desire to serve others. As you turn these pages, you'll find practical tools and reflective exercises that will not only enhance your leadership skills but also will inspire you to cultivate a deeper connection with yourself and those around you.

This book is a timely reminder that the most meaningful growth comes from being thoughtful—about our actions, our relationships, and the legacy we aim to leave behind. I invite you to embrace the journey ahead with an open heart and a reflective mind, knowing that the path to becoming a more thoughtful leader is one of the most rewarding endeavors you can undertake.

I have known Randy for well over ten years and have benefited from his thoughts and advice on leadership many times during our friendship. I write this foreword because I want to encourage you not just to read this book and put it aside. I recommend you keep it on your desk for a year or two, taking one or two chapters at a time and practicing Randy's advice for sixty days before moving on to the next.

Ti voglio bene!

—Andreas Widmer, Author of *The Art of Principled Entrepreneurship: Creating Enduring Value*

INTRODUCTION

Inspired by countless coaching conversations with leaders around the world and rich experiences from my thirty year-plus business career, I am excited to share *Becoming a More Thoughtful Leader*. My newest work is written through the prism of my self-reflective style to offer actionable best practices and helpful insights on a host of leadership topics. The book shares real experiences, candid observations, and hard-fought wisdom in each thought-provoking chapter that I believe you will find relevant for your life and career. The eclectic topics range from vulnerability to accountability to patience to addressing workplace disconnectedness . . . and much, much more.

You are encouraged to pause at the end of each chapter and reflect on a few questions or action steps to deepen both your understanding of the topic and motivate you to put into practice what you just learned. One of the key themes of the book is not only the subtle challenge to look in the mirror and be more thoughtful about your own growth as a leader, but also to be more thoughtful about investing in your work colleagues and others you encounter throughout the day. My hope is that the readers of this book will not only become better *leaders*, but also better and more thoughtful *human beings*.

What will you gain from reading this book? I found myself in a typical reflective mood as I sipped coffee in my home office in the wee hours before dawn one morning earlier this past summer and began to write this Introduction. These early-morning writing sessions often lead to blog posts or book chapters filled with actionable advice I humbly offer my network on ways to continue their own growth and encouragement to better serve those around them. This particular reflection time led me to identify and offer two distinct and simple "investment" challenges I hope you will consider taking on after you read the book.

Be Thoughtful about Investing in *Yourself*

How will you develop yourself ***professionally*** in the coming year?

- What helpful books are on your reading list?
- What helpful podcasts will you listen to?
- Is there training or development offered by your company or externally that will help you enhance your business knowledge or leadership skills?
- Have you considered asking for formal mentorship from leaders you respect and admire?
- Who will you seek candid feedback from regarding your current performance and areas to improve?
- Are you willing to get out of your comfort zone and take on new professional challenges this year?
- Which chapters in this book helped you identify opportunities for improvement? Are you

committed to implementing some of the ideas and best practices you read?

How will you grow **_personally_** in the coming year?

- What do you see when you look in the mirror?
- Have you identified what you want to get out of life? What are your personal goals—and are you on the right path to achieve them?
- Do you have clarity about your personal and professional priorities? Are they in the right order?
- How will you better practice self-care? Will you develop and commit to a doable plan to take better care of your mental, physical, and spiritual health?
- How will you invest more time in developing and nurturing relationships this year?
- How will you focus more time on the people and activities that bring you joy, happiness and fulfillment in the coming year?
- Are you self-aware? Do you know how you are showing up for others and how they may see you? Who can help you gain this candid insight and what changes do you need to make?

Be Thoughtful about Investing in *Others*

I am very grateful for a mindset I learned from my friend and fellow author Andreas Widmer that I encourage the readers of this book to adopt as soon as possible. He taught me the Italian phrase *Ti voglio bene* ("I want your good"). As you ponder the powerful simplicity of these words, consider the coming year and beyond as an opportunity to look around you at work, at home, and in your community through this lens. If you are thoughtful and truly seek the good for others, you will do your best to serve and help others in all areas of your life.

- Who can you mentor and help grow at work? How can you help them identify and maximize their talents? How will you apply the lessons in this book to teaching, coaching and guiding others?
- How can you contribute in a more meaningful way to helping produce a better product or service for your clients and customers (inside or outside your company)?
- What causes can you serve to make your community and the world a better place?
- How will your family, work colleagues, and friends experience the best of you and know you truly have their best interests and well-being at heart?

Who is this book written for? Everyone, regardless of their title or experience level, can benefit from making these two types of investments moving forward and utilizing the learnings from each chapter to enhance their efforts. As with most of my books, you can easily jump around and read the topics that interest you most. The numerous topics addressed in *Becoming a More Thoughtful Leader* will add to the richness, value, and impact of your growth and the growth of those around you. I can't promise this book has all the answers you seek, but reading and carefully reflecting on the content will provide a helpful spark for meaningful growth in your pursuit of excellence and more thoughtfulness in your approach to leadership and life.

Thoughtfully invest in *yourself* and *others* . . . let's keep it simple and have a shared goal of looking back at the end of the next year with gratitude for how much we have all grown and the positive difference we made in the lives of those around us. The ripple effect of these actions will make a significant and favorable impact on us, on the people we encounter each day, and hopefully on a world that desperately needs more thoughtful leaders.

I look forward to being your companion on this journey as you absorb the words in front of you.

Thank you for reading my book and aspiring to be a more thoughtful leader.

CHAPTER 1

Confessions of a High-Functioning Introvert

No matter what your perceived shortcomings or "deficits" may be, it is often possible to work around them, eliminate them, or turn them into strengths.

Decades ago when I was still in school, I used to feel anxious and uncomfortable around large groups of people. As I grew older, the obligatory networking events I was told to attend to benefit my career were especially difficult for me, and I often felt overwhelmed by the idea of meeting so many people at once, remembering their names, and knowing the perfect thing to say. As my titles and responsibilities expanded, there was a frequent expectation to present to my team and other employees as well as occasional invitations to speak outside the company, both of which filled me with dread. When I began writing books many years ago, the calls for public speaking increased exponentially, and the talks were typically followed by obligatory social time with talk attendees and signing books. This only added to my stress and anxiety.

I struggled in silence for many years. I worked as hard

as I could to meet these expectations and not let anyone know of my challenges. I spent long hours in preparation, often practicing elaborate mental role-playing to make sure I showed up well in group settings or developing long PowerPoint decks that covered every aspect of the topic I was speaking on to mask my presentation anxiety. I became an expert at how to make an appearance at networking events, say hello to a few key people, and then quietly leave. In retrospect, I was not being true to myself in this effort to project a confidence I did not feel and meet the expectations others were placing on me. I assumed that this shortcoming—this "deficit" of mine—was something I would wrestle with for the rest of my life.

In my mid-thirties, I formed a friendship with an industrial psychologist who was doing work with my company. When I confided to this insightful man about the challenges I was having, he had me take a battery of tests to gain more understanding about what I was facing. He helped me realize that I am, and likely always have been, a *high-functioning introvert*. I truly enjoy engaging with others, but my energy for people fades as the day goes on, and large groups of people can cause me to feel stressed and overwhelmed. He challenged me to turn this "deficit" of mine into a strength and find a more authentic path forward that better suited my personality. The light bulb came on for me as I began to stop seeing my challenges as liabilities or burdens and instead began to look on them as minor obstacles that could be worked around or eliminated. The process of **rethinking** my deficit began at this critical stage of my career.

Here are five fundamental shifts I made that I still employ more than twenty years later:

1. **Shifting from networking events to one-on-one coffee meetings and the occasional lunch.** I am very sharp and energized early in the morning, and I love getting to know individuals over coffee or a meal. This fits my style perfectly and promotes a conversational approach focused on vulnerability and authenticity. The result? Over the last two decades I have met (and continue to meet) thousands of people for coffee or lunch, and I've built solid relationships in a sustainable way that is much more effective than the stress-inducing cattle call of networking gatherings. This approach has also developed my active listening skills and passion for being curious, which are strengths I am grateful to use frequently in my daily life.

2. **Switching from only attending events to hosting events.** Rather than enduring the stress of attending the events of others where I don't know many people and am likely going to feel uncomfortable, I have learned to engage in different ways of meeting groups of people over the last two decades. I now host events with compelling guest speakers where I invite seventy-five to one hundred leaders I know well from my business network. I also put together small-scale coffees or lunches with four or five people from my business and personal friendship circles. These settings are much more comfortable for me, and my guests have shared they find them very valuable.

3. **Moving beyond decks to storytelling and facilitated Q&A.** In my professional work, I often utilize presentation decks as I work with teams and large cohorts of leaders, but I make the sessions very interactive, utilize breakout sessions, and share relevant stories rather than only read from text. When I am invited to give talks, I have largely scrapped the decks and share interesting stories from my life experiences and helpful ideas or tips the audience can utilize in their own lives. My favorite approach to speaking events is to have the person who extended the invitation sit with me at the head of the event space and ask me questions on whatever topics they desire, allowing time for the audience to do the same. This evolution in my speaking approach fits my personality well and has made me a much more effective and compelling speaker.

4. **Becoming a writer.** My industrial psychologist friend gave me a leather journal a few months into our friendship and encouraged me to start writing down my thoughts. He said I had a voice that needed to be heard and that focusing on writing as the medium to share that voice was a better fit for my personality than only doing speaking events. I was apprehensive, never having written a word for public consumption before, but I trusted his thoughtful advice and began to journal. More than twenty years later, I have filled two dozen journals, authored eleven books, and written hundreds of blog posts. I will be forever grateful to this wonderful friend who encouraged me to embrace what

has become such a meaningful and enjoyable part of my life.

5. **Managing my energy better.** I observed decades ago that I often felt flat and tired at the end of the workday. I learned, with my friend's help and the testing I referenced, that I needed to find ways to "recharge my battery" during the day to have adequate energy for myself and others. Here are the three changes I made that helped the most: 1) I get in thirty minutes (minimum) of exercise every day on my Peloton bike, typically over my lunch break if possible; 2) I schedule two thirty-minute blocks of "air" on my calendar spread four hours apart when I don't have any meetings; and 3) I walk two to four miles at the end of every day just before dinner, weather permitting. These important breaks on my calendar help me stay more energized throughout the day, and I am better able to give my clients, friends and family what they need and deserve from me.

You might think this chapter is about the struggles of a high-functioning introvert, but you would be missing the key point. No matter what your perceived shortcomings or "deficits" may be, it is often possible to work around them, eliminate them, or turn them into strengths. Think about areas you have been told to work on or have identified as challenges. There are certainly going to be some areas where you do need to improve, and we should all embrace growth and personal development, take part in helpful training, or seek mentors and coaches who can help us. But perhaps some areas of your life that are causing stress, anxiety, or worry simply require new thinking and a more *authentic approach* from you that better fits your needs and personal style.

After you read this chapter, I encourage you to make a list of any shortcomings or deficits you are wrestling with right now. Make a concerted effort to get help and development in the areas in which you truly want to improve, but also examine where you might just need to change your mindset and rethink how you view your deficits. Shift your approach, embrace your authentic self, and follow paths that may buck conventional wisdom and the chorus of opinions of those who simply want you to conform to the way everybody else does things. Seek the counsel of candid and wise people in your life who can help you in this effort. I know for a fact if I had not made the shift I did over two decades ago with the help of a wise friend, I would not be doing the work I love today or having the countless opportunities I am blessed with to serve my clients, friends, and community. Think carefully about how this topic speaks to you, be intentional about what changes you need to make, and enjoy the rewards I am confident you will experience.

Have you been able to identify any of your own deficits or shortcomings? How are you dealing with them? Do you feel stuck? Have you considered outside the box approaches like the ones I shared? This week, pick one area you want to improve on your own or with an accountability partner and brainstorm innovative ways to make improvements.

CHAPTER 2

Embracing a Once-Treasured Practice Can Make You More Memorable

Making the extra effort to say thanks in a genuine, personal manner goes a long way. It is pleasurable to do, and it encourages more of the same good behavior.

RICHARD BRANSON

I was having coffee with three friends not long ago, and we had an interesting discussion about the topic of gratitude—specifically, thank-you notes. I shared with them that I had recently received a wonderful handwritten thank you note from a mentee of mine. I shared how I knew this young professional, what development areas we were working on, and what specifically had prompted the note. When I finished, I asked each of them to share a little about the last handwritten thank-you note they had received and exactly how they felt when they received it.

What struck me as interesting was the warm smile each of them had as they described the note and who it was from, why they had received it, and the positive way the note made them feel. I then asked them to describe the last thank-you message they had received via email or text. The difference in their responses was markedly different. They were truly appreciative of the thank-you messages, but their descriptions were more perfunctory, and these messages were deleted along with the other emails or text messages they had received that day. It's also interesting to note that each of them said they keep the handwritten thank-you notes they receive. I practice the same habit and have a box full of them in my home office.

Why is this relevant? I have long shared with clients, friends, college students, and young professionals the importance and value of the handwritten thank-you note. I know it sounds old-fashioned, but this is one of the best ways to make a favorable impression on another person. Emailed and texted thank-you messages are nice, but they are soon deleted and forgotten. Handwritten notes are memorable. As I shared, I have kept every handwritten note I've ever received. Thank-you notes are special, and when I read them (and reread them), it makes me think warmly about the other person—which is really the whole point.

If you want to be viewed more positively than your colleagues at work as you look to advance in your career or fare better than others interviewing for jobs you are interested in, consider the power and impact of the simple handwritten thank-you note. I can share from experience and observation that the extra effort and thoughtfulness associated with this once-common tradition makes you stand out favorably in the eyes of the recipient. Wouldn't you like to have been one of the individuals positively discussed in the coffee meeting I mentioned with my friends, all of whom are senior business leaders?

Not everything is worthy of a handwritten thank-you note. In fact, the majority of the time, emailed and texted thank-you messages are more than sufficient (especially for employees of global companies). I certainly send my share of gratitude via email and text each week. We also should be consistently expressing our sincere thanks verbally and in the moment; that is hopefully a given. But every now and then, an impactful encounter, helpful conversation, or kind act will merit the investment of time in a heartfelt and thoughtful written note of gratitude sent in a timely manner.

What actually merits a handwritten thank you note? In my opinion, here are some relevant examples:

- After every first interview and if you accept a job offer
- When a busy senior leader makes time to meet with you to further your development
- If you receive a promotion or unexpected pay raise
- When you receive wise and impactful counsel from a work colleague or friend
- ALWAYS after receipt of an unexpected gift and all gifts received on your special days
- In response to any acts of kindness when someone has gone out of their way to do something special and helpful for you
- When someone commits a truly selfless act, shows courage, or demonstrates sincere care and concern for others (even if it didn't directly impact you)
- If you hear a great speaker or read something by an author that really inspires you

- To show your appreciation for the business partnership you have with customers and clients
- A few times a year, especially at Thanksgiving, to express how much you appreciate your employees and colleagues and to thank them for some specific aspect of their performance when appropriate

Seven Helpful Tips to Elevate Your Practice of Sending Handwritten Thank-You Notes

1. **Invest in quality stationary, personalized if possible.**
2. **Be specific.** Share exactly what prompted your note and why you are grateful.
3. **Be careful with spelling, grammar, and penmanship.** I know this is obvious, but be very careful with spelling, grammar, and neatness. You might ask someone you trust to proof your note if possible. A handwritten note that misses the mark in these areas can work against you and leave a poor impression. Idea: if you are concerned about your penmanship, you might try typing a short letter to include in your thank-you card and then sign the bottom of the note. Handwritten is always best, but I have seen this alternative, and it's a suitable replacement if necessary.
4. **Be a good detective and track down their address.** Corporate addresses are easily available online. If the individual works from home (this is obviously more common these days), politely ask them for their address and let them know you plan to follow

up. If this feels a little uncomfortable, reach out to their administrative assistant if they have one and ask for the address. Also, if you really want to make a positive impression on a senior leader, drop off the handwritten note in person at their office (if this is geographically possible).

5. **Have a goal of writing at least four handwritten thank-you notes per month.** If you are paying attention and acting with intention, you should be able to find appropriate reasons to send at least four handwritten thank you notes a month.

6. **Remember that this is a best practice regardless of your generation, experience level, or title.**

7. **Take a moment and consider how you will make the other person feel with your note.** This perspective goes beyond how it affects you. You are showing someone else gratitude and appreciation, and your note might just be the best thing that happens to them that particular day. A thoughtful thank-you note, therefore, can also be an act of kindness.

You may have decided that the whole idea of handwritten thank-you notes is too old-fashioned, a waste of time, or you are simply too busy. I understand and can appreciate your perspective. But you may also read this chapter and see the value of the concept—or maybe you already make this a regular practice. Perhaps you are reflecting right now on the written thank-you notes you have received in the past and the positive impressions they made on you. Maybe you are a little stuck and looking for a competitive edge to grow your career or a job seeker looking to distance yourself from the competition. Hopefully, you're seeing the best reason of all to send more thoughtful handwritten notes: *It is warmer, more personal, more meaningful, and clearly more memorable* than the email or texted thank-you messages that have been your primary go-to practice up until now.

One more thing: At the end of his section in Tim Ferriss's highly acclaimed and successful book *Tools of Titans*, author and marketing guru Seth Godin is asked, "Any final words of advice?" He says, "Send someone a thank-you note tomorrow."

Seth Godin could have left us with *anything*, but he chose this simple call to action to thoughtfully end his chapter. Godin is right, and I strongly encourage you to give it a try.

Send one handwritten thank you note this week to someone who fits the example checklist I shared or for some other reason you deem worthy. Reflect on how it made you feel. How do you think it made the recipient feel? Consider making this a practice at least four times a month going forward. You will be glad you did!

CHAPTER 3

How Do I Deal with an Identity Crisis after Leaving My Old Job?

There are better things ahead than any we leave behind.
C.S. LEWIS, *THE COLLECTED LETTERS
OF C.S. LEWIS*, VOLUME 3

Not long ago I received a question from a longtime friend that is similar to other questions I have been fielding for years about dealing with self-worth and identity issues after losing a job. My friend was part of a significant reorganization at his company several months ago and his senior leadership role was eliminated. He had been very successful in the position over the years and had devoted himself to the company and his team. He is also an exceptional husband and dad with a heart for serving the community.

After leaving his job, he made the most of this period to invest heavily in quality time with his family, wrote his first book, and stayed engaged with meaningful consulting work while seeking his next full-time role. He and his wife even bought a small franchise business as an investment. Six months later, he was still looking for a new job and reached out to me for guidance on how to deal with what he called a lingering *crisis of identity* about not being a senior executive leading a large team and all that comes with that responsibility.

With his enthusiastic permission, I am sharing my response here.

What you are facing is a very common challenge for a number of senior business leaders I know. When we are fortunate to enjoy success in our careers and hopefully do work we enjoy, losing our job can make us feel uncomfortable, unfulfilled, or worse. For many leaders, it can come down to understandable worry about finding a new job to support the family and maintain a lifestyle to which we have become accustomed. As you said in your situation, it also often can create a crisis of identity.

What you may be experiencing is an awareness that you had a lot of your self-worth and personal validation wrapped up in this last job. This is not unusual! You had a big role, built a great team, and enjoyed a lot of success. Losing that job has possibly created some doubts about who you are and your path forward. My encouragement to you is to recognize and connect more strongly than ever to your true priorities in life. Knowing you, they are likely God, family, health, relationships, and work in that order (or something similar). Over the last six months, you have been steadfast in your faith, given a ton of quality time to your loved ones, written an exciting new book that will change lives, engaged with a number of interesting people, and purchased a new business. All of these amazing faith, time, creative, and financial investments are seeds you are planting to build a bridge to a brighter future that will more than replace what you are missing from your old role.

My humble advice to you:

Be patient. You will eventually feel less anxious about leaving your old role as you see new opportunities open up for you. It takes time to find a new opportunity, sometimes as long as a year, and you are doing the right things that will help you identify and land a new position.

Trust in God's plan for your life. Consider St. Thomas More's famous quote: "Nothing can come but what God wills. And I am very sure that whatever that be, however, bad it may seem, it shall indeed be the best." Remember to be grateful for your challenges, not just your blessings.

What will be inscribed on your gravestone? Do you want to be remembered as a senior executive OR a great husband, father, man of faith, community servant, and someone who positively impacted the lives of everyone he met? We should never want our gravestone to read "He Had a Great Career." Let this idea reconnect you to a deeper understanding of where your identity, value, and self-worth truly reside.

Recognize all of this as a gift and be grateful. The last several months have been a gift to recalibrate your life, strengthen your already impressive personal foundation, and prepare for the next opportunity. Be grateful for this time and reflect on the lessons you have learned in the years ahead.

Lean on friends. You have friends and relationships

all over the country. Don't be afraid to ask them for assistance with your search, just as you are always willing to help and serve them. Don't let pride get in the way of activating a network of people who care for you and are more than willing to help.

Design your ideal personal life before your career life. Make sure the next role you choose conforms around the other more important priorities I shared earlier. Doing this will make you a better person, a better leader, and even more successful at work. You are good at this now, but be even more intentional with your next job.

The bottom line is you are *so much more* than your old job. With God's help, you have a built a values-based life filled with countless blessings. Every day that passes puts more distance between you and your old role. Savor this time, remember that your identity and self-worth is not defined by the work you do, and keep in mind that we should always *be working to live, not living to work.*

The response I shared with my friend may describe your situation or that of someone you know. Having an identity crisis when we lose our jobs is very real, and I have seen it countless times in my career. There are also very real financial stresses, which multiply the anxiety we may feel around finding a new role. There are helpful book and blog resources available on job search and excellent career coaches out there who can guide you if what I have written is not exactly what you need at this time.

Wherever you are on the career or job search journey, I wish you the best of luck.

HOW DO I DEAL WITH AN IDENTITY CRISIS?

Have you ever lost a job you loved? A job you poured your heart into for years? How did you feel in the weeks and months that followed? Does my friend's situation sound familiar? There is plenty of useful advice in this chapter for how to deal with the loss of a job, and I hope you find it helpful, but I also respectfully challenge you to seek out someone you know who is looking for a new role and connect with them over a meal or coffee. Take their emotional temperature. Are they having an identity crisis? Lean in and help them.

CHAPTER 4

The Power of Anointed Credibility

Few things can help an individual more than to place responsibility on him, and to let him know that you trust him.

BOOKER T. WASHINGTON

When my 2021 book, *Essential Wisdom for Leaders of Every Generation*, came out, I was asked to facilitate a town hall/ Q&A session for leaders and aspiring leaders of a well-known Atlanta company based on the book's content. I was invited to speak at the event by an old friend and senior leader I have known for many years, with whom I served on a nonprofit board for almost a decade. In the weeks leading up to the town hall, I actively engaged with a talented young protégé of my friend who had been introduced to me in the first planning discussion as the point person who would handle all the planning and logistics. This younger colleague was praised by my friend as talented, completely trustworthy, "a rising star in our company," and "one of our best," and although I saw little of my friend in the coming weeks, this younger colleague expertly steered me through the planning and event without a hitch. He did a fantastic job, and I hope we can work together again. What strikes me as interesting was the intentional approach my friend took. He elevated and praised a younger colleague to help me feel more at ease, gave this young leader an opportunity to shine, and effortlessly and subtly exited from most of the planning so he could focus on his more important executive responsibilities. I also now have faith and trust in this impressive young leader and feel invested in helping him succeed in the future.

Why is this important?

Consider this brief story an example of *anointed credibility*. This is an approach I have taken numerous times in my career when I recognized that my clients often wanted to work primarily with me, based on our past working relationship and because I carried a senior title. It was physically impossible for me to manage every aspect of the work my clients wanted from me and my teams, so I would always bring a more junior colleague along with me on a first meeting to discuss a new project or engagement.

These colleagues were bright, talented, seeking development, and looking to grow their careers. I had full faith in their abilities, but they were unknown to my often-skeptical clients. I "anointed" these more junior members of the team by making it clear to my clients I believed in them, trusted them, and knew they would do excellent work. *In essence, I was asking the client to trust my judgment.* Yes, I put my own credibility at risk in doing so, but at some point leaders have to be willing to take the chance to offer opportunities for their team members to grow and develop. Much like the outcome from the story about my friend and his younger colleague, as my clients began working with these junior colleagues, the outcomes were typically very good.

These aspiring leaders gained invaluable experiences, and I could focus on leading the business, developing new client relationships, and engaging in the more strategic aspects of my job.

If you are a leader looking to more intentionally embrace the anointed credibility approach, here are four thoughts to consider:

1. **Invest your time**. How well do you know your direct reports? The rest of your team? Do you know their capabilities and career aspirations? How much one-on-one time do they get from you? Putting forth team members for important growth opportunities and moments to shine is risky and difficult when you don't really know them. Make this time investment a priority.

2. **Practice discernment, clarity, and empowerment**. Discern who on the team is ready to step up and embrace this challenge. Be clear about your expectations and let them know you are available if needed, but empower them to do the work and define their decision-making rights.

3. **Delegate, develop, and let go.** Leaders who struggle to delegate will have difficulty with the *anointed credibility* concept. One way to get out of the weeds is to identify who can do the work (or be trained to do the work) you are currently doing and then trust them to do it. The best leaders are always developing themselves and those around them. By letting go of certain aspects of your work and giving others on the

team an opportunity to shine, you are contributing in a meaningful way to their development; this frees you up (as my good friend Brandon Smith says) to "work more on the business, not in the business."

4. **Diversify your thinking**. There is sometimes a tendency to primarily practice anointed credibility with those who look, think, and act just like us. I challenge you to expand the aperture of your thinking and diversify by seeking team members who may sometimes get overlooked for these kinds of opportunities or those who think outside the box.

While this chapter is primarily tilted toward leaders interested in more intentionally embracing the practice of anointed credibility, I encourage younger professionals looking to advance your careers to think carefully about what this topic might mean for you. In chapter four of my book *Essential Wisdom for Leaders of Every Generation*, I wrote in detail about the importance of professional credibility and how to earn it. What this chapter offers is another path forward in gaining credibility, but you should first ask yourself the following questions and carefully reflect on your answers:

- Am I willing to do what it takes to learn and grow?
- Will I do more than just the minimum requirements and give that little extra that leaders may recognize and reward?
- Do I ask for more responsibility, volunteer for projects and tasks, and seek opportunities to prove myself?
- Do I have a strong work ethic?

- Have I sought out time with my boss and other senior leaders to learn from them, be curious about their career experiences, build trusting relationships, and seek their advocacy for opportunities?

Meet your leader(s) at least halfway. Don't wait in silence to be asked to do more. Sometimes you have to raise your hand and express your interest. Be comfortable with the idea that you must often earn the right to get opportunities—remember that nothing meaningful comes our way without hard work. The clear payoff is your own growth and development, accelerated career success, and increased self-confidence.

I have great faith in the generations joining the workforce and believe we should all do more to help them. They may think and act differently, but these younger colleagues are our future senior leaders, and it is vitally important they are successful. We, who may be from older generations, have an obligation to mentor them, train them, develop their leadership skills, and provide them with opportunities to shine. The intentional practice of anointed credibility is a proven and necessary approach to helping these junior and aspiring leaders with a leg up . . . the same leg up we may have been offered along the way in our careers. I know I benefited significantly as a young professional when senior leaders helped me and offered me opportunities the way I have described in this chapter.

Here is my respectful challenge to you: In the coming weeks, look for at least two meaningful opportunities to offer anointed credibility to junior members of your team. Set them up for success with an internal or external client, make it clear these junior members have your trust and support, give clear direction, empower them . . . and get out of the way. I promise you will survive, and most importantly, your younger colleagues will gain invaluable lessons, practical experience, and increased confidence.

Have you ever personally benefited from anointed credibility in your career? How did it help you? Is this a regular practice for you today with your newer colleagues? Embrace the challenge in the last paragraph and make this a regular part of your leadership approach.

CHAPTER 5

Reflecting on a Gift from a Thoughtful Friend

I appreciate that my friend's traditional, old-school example speaks to a need for all of us to perhaps be a little more human in our dealings with one another.

A friend of mine has mailed me clippings of articles on a number of business, cultural, and historical topics over the past ten years from the *Wall Street Journal* and various magazines that he thinks will interest me. He always adds a handwritten personal note of greeting and briefly points out what I will find interesting about the topic he has shared. I know he does this for others in his circle, and I am extremely grateful to have a thoughtful friend like this in my life.

Early one morning while reading his latest literary share, it occurred to me that this is a friend who has taken the time to get to know me over the years. He is curious, keenly observant, and a very good listener. He has a sincere desire to add value to his friendships and embraces an old-school method to share his gifts with others. His effort and time investment in cutting out the articles, writing the notes, and physically mailing them to friends speaks to someone who is generous, thinks deeply about others, and is proudly countercultural. *I often reflect on how much I aspire to be more like my friend, but know I fall short.*

Think about how often we respond to a kindness or service done for us with a perfunctory "thanks/thx" via email or text instead of calling or sending a handwritten note of gratitude. How often do we opt for staring into the abyss of our iPhone screens instead of engaging in thoughtful conversation? How often do we neglect to be curious and truly listen to the people we know, better understand them, and know what is going in their lives? Do we take the time to reflect and think more deeply about our friends and work colleagues? How can we add more value to these relationships, show our appreciation, and perhaps serve them better?

I found these reflection questions to be convicting. I am not a Luddite, and I embrace the appropriate use of technology, but I appreciate that my friend's traditional, old-school habit speaks to a need for all of us to perhaps be a little more human in our dealings with one another. Technology has its uses, but it will never replace a smile, a hug, a kind word, or a thoughtful handwritten note. I know busyness is my typical excuse—and it is a very *poor* excuse indeed.

I have decided to be patient and give myself a little grace on this topic as I realize it will take time to make such a change. I am sincerely committed to do better and will begin in the coming weeks to be more mindful of opportunities to focus on more personal and human ways to thoughtfully engage with my network. I will ask trusted friends and family members to hold me accountable to this higher standard I wish to achieve . . . *and I will start by sending a handwritten thank you note to my thoughtful friend.*

How does this brief chapter speak to you? The key theme is to thoughtfully engage in a more human way with those around us. Technology has its uses, but emails, texts, and looking at screens can be cold ways to communicate. Pick two people at work or in your personal life before the end of the week to more thoughtfully engage with and consider making this a regular practice going forward.

CHAPTER 6

Respecting Boundaries: An Invitation to Look in the Mirror

One of the most stress-inducing challenges any of us can experience is never being able to turn work off.

I am certain readers of this chapter will agree we all need adequate time to rest, recharge, and focus on our families and lives outside of work. Even if it is only an aspiration at this point in your career, my hope is that no matter what your age, you will focus on working to live and not living to work. Unfortunately, workplace stress, burnout levels, and quiet quitting are at all-time highs according to the 2023 *Gallup State of the Global Workplace Report*. We have a tangible problem in the workplace today, and *lack of respect for boundaries is a key contributor.*

Over the past several months, there has been a noticeable uptick in the number of conversations I've had with professionals in my network seeking guidance on how to deal with bosses and other work colleagues not respecting boundaries around personal time. There are countless helpful blog posts and book resources on setting boundaries for ourselves, but let's look at this from a different angle. I would like to offer guidance in this chapter that asks all of us to look in the mirror and honestly assess if we are guilty of not respecting boundaries—and how we can course correct.

The Problem

I would like to narrow our focus to the most typical complaint I hear from professionals I know: receiving emails and calls after hours during the week, over the weekend, and during vacations. One of the most stress-inducing challenges any of us can experience is never being able to turn work off. We work all day, which can be stressful enough, but inevitably the emails start coming in after hours when we are having dinner with our families, exercising, or enjoying time with friends or loved ones. Maybe we are just savoring some alone time.

Receiving work emails or calls over the weekend or during vacation is even worse. We have gotten through a long work week and are looking forward to the opportunity to do things we enjoy, get some rest, or focus on family activities when the emails and calls come in. Maybe we are on a vacation trip when work invades, and we lose the opportunity to rest and recharge. Our families and loved ones suffer as well as we are pulled away from time with them to handle work issues.

You can rightly think that we all have the right to **just say no** . . . to ignore emails and calls after hours. We do indeed have that right, and I address this squarely in chapter 10 of my 2022 book *Upon Reflection* titled "How to Identify and Thwart Time Thieves (and Not Become One)," which I encourage you to read. But I want the emphasis of this chapter to address why some of our colleagues and senior leaders don't respect boundaries and how we can encourage positive changes.

Five Key Reasons Boundaries Are Not Respected

1. **The fluid work schedules of remote and hybrid team members.** The old nine-to-five workday largely disappeared for many of us during the COVID pandemic. Colleagues who work remotely or hybrid often have poorly defined work hours with no clear start and end to their workday, which leads others to assume they can reach out anytime.

2. **The Badge of Honor.** I have observed over my career the misplaced praise we give team members "doing whatever it takes" and never turning work off in order to advance their careers. This mindset sometimes ignores the heavy price being paid for such a commitment and how it might affect other work colleagues. There is nothing wrong with hard work, but working smarter and more efficiently during the established workday is just as important as working hard. Our desire to wear the "badge" should never negatively impact others.

3. **Inefficient use of time during the day.** I have written extensively on improving time management, and I am confident in sharing that one of the biggest contributors to lack of respect for boundaries comes from *wasted time*. The primary culprit in our inefficiency is dysfunctional meetings that are often repetitive, missing agendas, have no assigned task ownership, and lack accountability with deadlines. Our days are often filled with such meetings. When we struggle to get everything done during the

typical workday, the growing (and often unspoken) assumption is we will do it nights and weekends, leading colleagues, bosses, and other leaders to invade that time with follow-up communication.

4. **Procrastination and poor planning.** How often in your career have you received a message at the end of the workday, after hours, or late Friday afternoon regarding an urgent project deadline or last-minute presentation that is due the next day or on Monday? *Maybe you have even sent such a message to colleagues.* There are certainly legitimate instances when this will occur, but in my candid conversations over the years, I often have discovered these last-minute requests stem from procrastination or poor planning. The issues at hand often could have been addressed earlier or been anticipated to avoid impacting the valuable personal time of our colleagues.

5. **A very common excuse.** One of the most common excuses I hear is, "Just because I sent the email after hours or over the weekend, it doesn't mean they have to respond." Of course people feel they have to respond! To not respond puts them at risk for being perceived as not engaged or not being team players. Even if they don't respond, they are likely interrupting their personal time to read it. We all have the right to work when and how we wish, but just because we want to get work off our plate at 8:00 p.m. at night or on Saturday mornings, this does not give us the right to create unnecessary stress for our colleagues and appropriate their well-earned personal time.

I hope you have read these five points and looked in the mirror. I know I have been guilty of some of these in the past. Does respecting boundaries sound like an area where you need to make some changes? If not, do you have colleagues who could benefit from this chapter? What are positive steps to help yourself or others better respect boundaries?

Consider These Five Practical Approaches

1. **Rethink what urgent really means.** Before you call or email a colleague after hours, evaluate if it can wait. Is it really urgent enough to justify invading the precious off time of a teammate? Will the business come to an end if you don't email the team at 8:00 p.m. about an upcoming project deadline? Does the client issue actually need to be dealt with at 9:00 p.m. at night? Some things—*most things*—can wait until the next day. Use better discernment and remember that if everything is urgent, than nothing is urgent.

2. **Make use of delayed send for emails.** If you use Outlook, there is an easy way to delay the delivery of emails to the next day or on Monday. This gives you the freedom to work when you like but not deliver the messages until normal work hours. This one step, if consistently utilized, makes a tremendous difference in respecting boundaries.

3. **Relentlessly focus on time efficiency.** What if we all focused on making better use of our time? Each of us can plan our days better, run more efficient meetings (and expect others to do the same), better anticipate and deal with issues in advance, and ensure our colleagues (and

we) have enough time during the day to get our jobs done. If we make significant progress in time efficiency, we will see a positive ripple effect that will reduce stress and improve the quality of life outside of work.

4. **Respect, empathize, and practice *Ti voglio bene*.** We sometimes can have blinders on at work. We get so focused on the task, project, or latest emergency that we may forget we are in a community of our fellow human beings. These fellow humans have unique physical and mental needs, lives outside of work, people they care about, weaknesses and strengths, etc. All of us, especially those who are privileged to be leaders, have a responsibility to show respect and empathy to our colleagues. We have a further responsibility to practice *Ti voglio bene*, which I shared is Italian for "I want your good." We should always want what is best for all our teammates. Protecting boundaries is best fueled by respect, empathy, and wanting what is best for others.

5. **Model it.** Be the role model for others. Set good and healthy boundaries for yourself and honor the boundaries of everyone around you. The only behavior you can really control is your own.

Stress, burnout, and disengagement are all significant issues for today's workforce. My encouragement is to evaluate whether we are negatively adding to these issues or helping to solve them. For the good of our colleagues, our companies, and ourselves, let's be open to making changes when necessary.

It's simply the right thing to do—and everybody wins when boundaries are respected.

Do a quick gut-check: How are you doing at respecting the boundaries of your work colleagues? Do the reasons offered as to why boundaries are not respected resonate with you? Utilize the best practices in this chapter and begin this week to make improvements. Are others violating your time boundaries? Respectfully engage with them and share the relevant lessons you have just learned.

CHAPTER 7

Workspace Matters

I love my job, but I especially love doing my work in this special workspace . . .

One day I received an email from a former coaching client with whom I worked in 2019. The email simply read: "I can't thank you enough for the helpful advice. I made a lot of the changes you recommended, and it has made a significant difference in my mood and how I think about work. Much appreciated!" He was referring to a Zoom call we had some time ago in which we caught up on life, family, and work. He shared that he was feeling burned out with work and unmotivated, which was negatively affecting his family relationships and overall mental outlook. He is a senior executive with a well-known Atlanta-based company who splits time between his corporate office, a home office in his basement, and a moderate travel schedule. I was asking him a number of questions about the stress and pressure he was feeling when I suddenly noticed the stark white, undecorated walls of his home office behind him. Going with a hunch, I asked him to describe in great detail the room he was in.

He seemed surprised by my question, but shared that his

basement office had a desk and chair, nothing on the walls, a few books, no photos, and a window looking into his backyard. He said he used the office for work and nothing else . . . and his office at the corporate headquarters also mirrored this minimalist style. He asked me why I was interested, and in response I shared a detailed description of my own home office.

In contrast to his, my office has comfortable furniture (including my favorite reading chair) and is filled with dozens of my favorite books, several pictures of my wife and sons from our most memorable moments, framed maps of some of my favorite places, items my sons made when they were in school or bought for me over the years, crucifixes and religious art, and framed covers of the books I have written. The walls of my office—this *sanctuary*, as I sometimes call it—are painted in warm colors, and everything about the room is inviting, comforting, and deeply personal for me.

When not visiting with clients at their offices or in restaurants, I do most of my work in this room. Thousands of meaningful conversations with clients, friends, and family have occurred within this special place. Almost all of my books and blog posts have been written in this space, and it is where I feel most creative, peaceful, and thoughtful. I love my job, but I especially love doing my work in this special workspace within my home. When I am stressed, feeling deflated, struggling with writer's block, or seeking motivation, I often only need to cast my eyes to the precious memories represented by the pictures and objects scattered around this room to course-correct and get back on track.

Why does this matter? Back to my former client and his dilemma . . .

The burnout he was feeling certainly has a number of causes, and this is not the only answer, but I encouraged him to do something about his work environment. I told him the detailed description of my own home office and the joy and comfort it gave me could serve as an example he could follow. The drab spaces at home and the corporate office he was working in were adding to his stress, lack of motivation, and overall burnout. He didn't enjoy or feel comforted and inspired by the spaces he was working in (where he spent several hours a day), and I pointed out that this was an easy area to address which would likely have significant positive impact on the challenges he shared.

He took my advice, and with his family's help, He incorporated the rich memories of his life through pictures and other personal things that mattered to him into his home office and did something similar at his other office. He sent me a picture of the dramatically different office spaces along with his email, and I hope this change continues to bring him the same level of satisfaction my office brings me on a daily basis.

It doesn't matter where you are in your professional life to begin imagining a better workspace for yourself. New college graduates just getting started to mid-career professionals to senior executives all have an opportunity to create an environment around them that inspires, motivates, and comforts. Whether you work from home, sit in a cube, or have your own company office, a few pictures, favorite books, a plant, beautiful art, or treasured mementos can be the little spark of inspiration or source of comfort you need when you are feeling discouraged, stressed, or unmotivated.

Four Thoughts to Consider if You Are Drawn to This Idea:

1. **Do what works for you!** Make your environment personal and memorable. Fill it with things that matter to you and will bring you joy, comfort, or inspiration when you need it.

2. **Use discernment.** When addressing your cube space or corporate office, be mindful of company policies. These are generally not overly restrictive, but play by the rules (if there are any). This also applies to what appears behind you on screen if you work from home and do a lot of virtual calls. Just use common sense, and if you're not sure, get feedback from a candid colleague on your chosen decoration. Be authentic but smart.

3. **Use it as a great conversation starter**. Not only will you personally benefit in multiple ways from personalizing your workspace, but you also will initiate new levels of conversation with work colleagues as they comment on your pictures or other personal items. A personalized workspace is similar to extending a friendly invitation into your world outside of work. Others will hopefully see your efforts as authentic and vulnerable, both of which are foundational in building trusting relationships.

4. **Remember that we live in challenging times.** If you are struggling with stress, anxiety, burnout, or any other aspect of mental health, the answers you may need likely will go well beyond your workspace. Don't

hesitate to get the help you need. The theme of this chapter is simply one helpful step of many to make work more enjoyable in these challenging times.

Some of the most fulfilled, joyful, and successful people I have encountered in my life pay careful attention to their environment and surround themselves at work in their own unique ways with the suggestions I have shared in this chapter. In the coming week, reflect on your own work environment. Based on this chapter, could you also stand to make some changes? Give it a shot, and I think you will appreciate the results.

Take stock of your workspace for the next few minutes or when you get back to your office. Based on this chapter, how does it look? Does it bring you joy? Help you be more productive? Make a quick list of things you would like to change and commit to get them done over the next thirty days.

CHAPTER 8

Are You Having the Right Accountability Conversations?

Are you holding others accountable for the right things? Look in the mirror and ask yourself if there is a possibility you have been unknowingly reinforcing the very behavior you wish to change . . .

In my professional work, I often look for interesting patterns of behavior and recurring themes. I was reflecting recently on a conversation I had with a former senior executive coaching client who reached out for advice about a direct report on her team who was promoted at the beginning of the year. Among other things, this direct report was struggling with delegation, operating in the weeds, and failing to empower his team. He is a doer and hands-on leader with a track record of getting results through his own efforts, but he was struggling to let go and was not known as a developer of people. He defined his success through getting things done, even if it meant doing much of the work himself. His boss, however, defined success through team performance and personal growth.

Having dealt with many similar situations and conversations like this over the last several years, I asked this senior leader to describe in detail the types of one-on-one conversations she was having with her direct report. She described the typical business review where they discussed how he was doing, progress on attainment of goals he was responsible for, how she could support him better, and overall business results. They occasionally had personal conversations, but she admitted she rarely said anything to him about delegating more. She shared that this somewhat generic conversation was fairly typical in their one-on-one meetings and that she had seen little change in his behavior since he began reporting to her.

Why is this relevant?

This conversation theme has caught my attention of late because too often we unknowingly enable less-than-desirable behavior and poor performance in our team members by the quality and content of the conversations we have in our one-on-one meetings. *Leaders should hold team members accountable for the behavior and performance they expect, and sometimes this requires a subtle but important shift in the accountability dialogue between leader and team member.* To put it simply, leaders should be very clear and specific about the outcomes they seek if they want behavior changes. If the same old conversations are getting the same old results, it's time for a change. Here is what I encouraged the senior executive to do in their one-on-one meetings going forward:

- Only discuss how the team is doing and the success they've attained instead of focusing on the team member's individual achievements.
- Ask for specific examples of how the team member was empowering the team and coaching them to success.

- Ask him to share, with specifics, how members of his team were executing on projects. Consider asking his team members to directly present to her on their projects and/or doing skip levels to hear from the team about how they are doing.
- Ask how the team member was developing each of his direct reports. Was he aware of their needs and career goals? Give him a reasonable window of time to create development plans for his direct reports and be ready to discuss them.
- If he attempts to shift the conversation back to his personal efforts, keep the focus on the team.
- Don't make any overt statement about the change in your approach. Just do it in an authentic and natural way.
- Consistently keep this pattern up and observe if the behaviors of the direct report begin to match the recent shift in conversation expectations.

I touched base with this former client again four weeks later to follow up and see how things were going. She was extremely pleased with the changes she was seeing in her direct report, but she honestly felt surprised that this simple shift in the dialogue could have such a dramatic impact. I shared that in my experience as both an executive coach of senior leaders and former senior executive, we all typically tend to conform our daily actions around what we perceive as the expectations and priorities of our boss.

Think about it . . .

She was asking him about what *he* was doing, what *he* was

working on, and how *he* was going to achieve his goals. She assumed he knew she wanted the team to do more and be fully engaged, but the language she used reinforced his natural tendencies to be in the weeds and reluctance to delegate. He had not really been asked to develop his people before now and struggled to do it. When she began making the conversation all about the team's efforts, his empowerment of the team, and how he was developing those he leads, he was able to shift his performance into a different gear and began bringing the team along with him. He modified his behavior and the way he approached his role to meet the new and clearer expectations of his boss. My former client said he quickly shifted from a manager who got things done to becoming one of the best *people leaders* on her direct team. This is a true story, and I have seen it played out numerous times over the years.

If you are a leader reading this chapter, reflect on the performance gaps on your team and carefully consider how you are engaging with your team members. Are you holding them accountable for the right things? Look in the mirror and ask yourself if there is a possibility you have been unknowingly reinforcing the very behavior you wish to change through your conversations. The sample conversation talking points I shared earlier can be modified for almost any performance issue and are not just for delegation, empowerment, and people development issues. Talk clearly and specifically about the outcomes you want and you are more likely to get them.

Take a minute and reflect on the individual performances of each member of your team and

*your recent conversations with them. Are you holding
them accountable for the right behaviors based
on this chapter? If not, try the above approach and
begin to shift the dialogue to address the behaviors
you are seeking. Keep track of when you shifted the
conversations and how long it takes to see positive
results.*

CHAPTER 9

A Practical (and Often Overlooked) Exercise to Help You Accelerate Your Career

Self-reflection is the school of wisdom.

BALTASAR GRACIAN, SPANISH JESUIT WRITER AND PHILOSOPHER

One Tuesday morning a few months before the publication of this book, I changed my early morning routine and went for a long walk after my coffee instead of at the end of the day. As I was walking, I thought about topics to write about for this book and reflected on the numerous conversations I had with clients and friends in my network in the preceding weeks. *What did I learn? What challenges are top of mind with this group? Are there consistent themes?* A number of ideas popped into my mind, but one topic in particular truly seemed universal and helpful to explore: *Our calendar is a great source of learning that we often overlook.*

As you have likely gleaned from my previous books and other writings, I am a reflective person. I'm always interested in extracting gold from encounters with others and often mine my past experiences and memories for valuable lessons that will help me grow and learn. As I was writing this chapter, I was struck by how often I encourage my clients (as I have for many years) to reflect carefully on past meetings and conversations with their colleagues as a helpful source of information on how to develop themselves. Specifically, I ask them to begin each workday by honestly reflecting on all of the people interactions from the previous day's calendar and slowly ponder their answers to these questions:

- How did I show up in each of these meetings or conversations?
- Did I model the behavior I would like to see in others?
- Did I show up as authentic? As appropriately personal and vulnerable?
- Was I fully present or distracted and multitasking?
- Was I organized and prepared for the conversation(s)?
- Did I ask good questions? What did I learn?
- Did I help, add value, and invest in my colleagues?
- What worked well that I wish to continue doing and what do I need to change?

You may think this is very basic and simple, and you would be correct. But I am surprised how rarely businesspeople do this helpful reflective exercise. Think of all the missed opportunities to learn and grow! What gets in the way of this being more commonplace? In my experience, *complacency, fear of looking in the mirror,* and *busyness* are typically the culprits.

Practical Application

Try this reflective exercise for a few weeks and see if it works for you. Be intentional and disciplined about carving out twenty to thirty minutes each morning to do it. Be brutally honest. Take careful notes on the answers to your questions. Continue doing what is working and seek help in areas you need to improve. Read helpful blog posts or books to enhance your knowledge and understanding. Seek coaching from colleagues who excel where you have opportunities to get better. Get accountability partners to help you make changes and stick to them. Always be willing to seek candid feedback from colleagues on your progress.

As you get more and more comfortable with this reflective approach, add an *additional and logical step*. Spend a few minutes at the beginning of each workday reviewing the upcoming day's calendar (or perhaps each Monday for the entire week). Think carefully about what is required of you in each meeting. How can you take the learnings from your calendar reflection exercises and apply them going forward? How do you need to show up? How will you best prepare? How will you add value? How will you maximize each meeting to be efficient with your time and energy? A helpful tip is to put your preparation notes into your calendar to ensure maximum readiness.

Are you on track at work? Everyone, from the newest team member to the CEO, should always be asking themselves these questions: *Is something missing? Am I truly self-aware about my strengths and weaknesses? Am I growing at a pace that fits my goals? Am I effective? Adding value?* Everybody has a different way of learning, and you should pursue the approach that works for you. But, if you are seeking a practical and proven method of looking in the mirror and reaching your potential, these reflective exercises really work, and I encourage you to give them a try.

There are plenty of action items contained in this chapter, but I would ask you to pause for a moment and think more deeply about this idea of reflecting on yesterday's activities. We are often racing at breakneck speed into the future, with little regard for learning helpful lessons from where we have been. How did you do? What do you need to change?

CHAPTER 10

What I Have Learned from Being an Expert at Only One Thing

As a single footstep will not make a path on the earth, so a single thought will not make a pathway in the mind. To make a deep physical path, we walk again and again. To make a deep mental path, we must think over and over the kind of thoughts we wish to dominate our lives.

WILFERD ARLAN PETERSON, *THE ART OF LIVING DAY BY DAY*

Malcolm Gladwell, in his 2008 bestseller *Outliers: The Story of Success*, argues that to achieve world-class expertise in any skill, you need about ten thousand hours of practice . . . deliberate, focused, and purposeful practice. This is an interesting premise, frequently debated, that occupied my thoughts this past summer when I received a question via email from a young professional I mentor about what I considered my areas of "expertise." As I wrote this chapter, I reflected on my answer, crafted through the lens of Mr. Gladwell's observation.

The following is a more fleshed-out version of the answer I sent my mentee.

It has occurred to me that I have accumulated more than ten thousand hours of focused practice in a number of areas of my life. I have been married for almost thirty years, a father for almost twenty-seven years, and a business leader for more than thirty-five years. But I don't consider myself an expert in any of these important roles. I don't say that out of false humility, but from the recognition that I have always felt I am a work in progress and an eager student in each area. To say I am an expert husband, father, or leader would seem laughable to me.

There is, however, one thing I believe I have achieved expertise in over the years. *I am an expert at taking long walks.* You must think I am joking, but indulge me for a few minutes. I have been a fan of taking long walks most of my adult life, and about twenty years ago I committed to daily walks assuming fair weather and good health. I love walking in the woods, on trails near my home, and in all the beautiful places my family and I have been fortunate to visit over the years. Being an expert at taking long walks may not seem like much of an achievement, but it is not simply the walking itself that I want to share with you. Aside from the obvious benefits to my health, stress relief, and the quiet time my high-functioning introvert personality craves, my life has been transformed by *what* I do while I am taking my walks.

I have one hard rule I follow when walking: no iPhones, no music, no podcasts, etc. Aside from exercise, I utilize my walking time to *think, pray,* and *reflect.* That's it. Because of this disciplined and somewhat monastic approach to walking, I have developed a number of best practices and harvested a great deal of fruit from my daily efforts. Here are seven areas of my life that are enriched through my deliberate and purposeful walks:

1. **Teaches me to savor solitude and quiet.** We are surrounded by unhealthy noise from social media, TV, and radio that I am able to eliminate while on my walks. I am fully engaged with people the majority of each workday through my coaching and consulting work. I spend meaningful time with my family and friends. I truly love all of these encounters, but my personality increasingly requires quiet time as I get older. I have learned to savor the quiet moments on the walking trail, and it has become a welcomed addiction I look forward to each day, one that refuels me to show up more engaged and energized with the people in my life.

2. **Strengthens my marriage.** I often think of my wonderful wife while walking and how to show up better as a husband and partner to this woman I love. Marriage is an investment . . . one of the greatest investments you can make . . . and I prioritize strengthening and growing my commitment to her every chance I get.

3. **Helps me to be a better father.** Just as I prioritize thinking about my wife and our marriage, I think a lot about being a better father. I am far from perfect and feel like I am still learning how to fill this vital role just as my sons are learning to make their way in the world. Reflecting on the walking trail about fatherhood has taught me to work hard at modeling the right behavior, be vulnerable enough to admit mistakes, ask for forgiveness, and practice forgiveness

toward them as well. I hope we all continue learning from one another in a loving way for the rest of our lives.

4. **Teaches me how to deal with adversity.** I reflect a great deal on challenges in my life and how to better handle adversity. The peace and quiet provided by my walks stimulates deeper thinking, creative problem solving, and has forced me to learn patience. Any burden I carry with me on a walk is typically much lighter by the time I am finished.

5. **Fosters deeper gratitude.** One of my favorite practices during a walk is to reflect on what and who I am grateful for in my life. Just reflecting on the blessings I have received and recognizing that sometimes struggles are a form of blessing to be grateful for has transformed my life. I credit these long treks as the catalyst for my deepening sense of gratitude—and for this I am grateful!

6. **Helps me to realize my career purpose.** Many years ago, I began to realize that my purpose and mission is not to solely focus on becoming a great leader and climb to the top of the corporate ladder, but to work at being a true *servant leader*. I think a lot in these quiet moments on the trail about better serving those around me through my coaching, writing, consulting, and speaking engagements. I have come to truly understand in a profound and meaningful way that the best way to *lead* others is by *serving* them.

7. **Strengthens my prayer life and faith.** I pray a great deal, especially on my daily walks. There is something

about being outside to experience God's creation and beauty that stimulates my desire to pray, seek His guidance, and be grateful for my blessings. I can't imagine where I would be as a man of faith without this focused time dedicated to prayer and reflection.

That's why I've chosen taking long walks as my solitary area of expertise. I have given this area of my life well over Mr. Gladwell's prescribed ten thousand hours of deliberate practice, and although I'm sure there are better experts than me when it comes to taking walks, I feel humbled and fortunate to have learned how to make the most of these special moments on the trail. The nurturing and growth I have experienced during my "practice" hours has transformed me and shaped who I have become.

I am still a work in progress, but I plan to keep on walking . . . *and learning* . . . as long as I am able.

Think about when you have experienced deep learning and powerful lessons in your life. Where were you? Who were you with? What were you doing? Even if you don't yet have Gladwell's ten thousand hours of practice in any specific area of your life, where do you feel you have developed strengths? Expertise? How are you positively using these gifts and talents of yours to help others?

CHAPTER 11

Let's Talk More about Opportunity

*Success in business requires training and discipline and hard work.
But if you're not frightened by these things, the opportunities are just
as great today as they ever were.*

DAVID ROCKEFELLER, FORMER CHAIRMAN AND CEO
OF CHASE MANHATTAN CORPORATION

I was speaking with a senior executive friend recently about the challenges of attracting, motivating, and retaining talent in her company. She described at great length the generous benefits and perks offered by her organization to future and current employees—it actually was a bit overwhelming to consider all someone would receive if they currently worked for or joined her company. This conversation was similar to others I've had with various senior leaders, and it reminds me that the war for talent has been raging for years. It is understandable that companies are increasingly getting more creative and aggressive in trying to attract and keep good people, but I believe we may be overlooking the most important benefit and perk of all: We should be talking more about *opportunity*.

What I'm about to share is a bit countercultural and will probably make some of you uncomfortable. I know there are exceptions, but it seems as if corporate America has been engaging in an unsustainable contest for several years now to outdo one another with ever more generous benefits and perks for future and current employees that is spiraling out of control. The current uncertain trajectory of the economy and increasing corporate layoffs will likely force companies to rein in benefits and perks somewhat, but the essential problem of how we think about attracting, motivating, and retaining talent will remain.

What are the consequences? This way of thinking contributes to an entitlement culture that certainly exists beyond the workplace, where the more we give, the more people expect—with no end in sight. This entitlement mentality can sometimes lead to a lack of appreciation from employees for what is being given to them or done for them. It can contribute to thinking *You are lucky to have me* instead of *I am lucky to be here*. I am suggesting that we have over-indexed on this so much that we may have forgotten the importance of simply discussing and selling *opportunities*. You will earn, learn, achieve, attain . . . *if* you work hard, perform well, make a commitment, and so on. For example:

- The **opportunity** to be compensated well for producing consistent results
- The **opportunity** to potentially earn stock with performance and tenure
- The **opportunity** to move up quickly based on attitude, hard work, and performance
- The **opportunity** to be developed, mentored, and grown by leaders and the company
- The **opportunity** to create, support, or sell products or services that will make a positive difference in the world

- The **opportunity** to be part of something special and help build a world-class organization

Of course, today's talent landscape may require us to offer competitive salaries, aggressive bonuses, and attractive healthcare or PTO plans, but those are *table stakes* and follow the demands of the marketplace and the whims of the economy. If we better promote the idea of opportunities and what it will take to achieve those opportunities, we will likely attract a higher-caliber candidate who is self-motivated, hardworking, and driven to succeed . . . a candidate who is eager to learn and grow. This type of candidate will be grateful for the benefits and perks, but even more grateful for the clear opportunity to excel and prove themselves. Overall, this candidate will likely be more appreciative of the opportunities placed in front of them and more likely to be a long-term member of the team if the company honors its commitments.

I am reminded of my first three corporate jobs in the first twenty-five years of my career before I launched my executive coaching company in 2012. My first job out of college as a manager trainee with a national retailer promised me excellent training, fast career growth, and a solid income opportunity if I worked hard and showed initiative. True to their word, I made the most of this opportunity and grew to a senior operational leadership role.

My second job as a director of recruiting with a national restaurant chain began with this promise in the interview from my future boss: "This will be the toughest job you have ever had, but you will have the opportunity to learn more here about people, leadership, and business than any job you will ever have and grow in ways you never thought possible." And it truly was the toughest job I ever had and stretched me in often uncomfortable ways, but I am grateful for all that I learned before leaving after four years as the vice-president of people and an officer of the company.

My final corporate role was with a national executive search firm that hired me as managing partner. The opportunity this firm offered was quite different. I would have the opportunity to earn an uncapped income based on performance, work with well-respected servant leaders who led the firm, and make a positive difference in the lives of our clients, candidates, and the community. All of this was true (and more) when I left as a partner and shareholder of this wonderful organization thirteen years later to start my own coaching and leadership development company.

I look back over my career with great appreciation for all the opportunities I have been given and the chances to prove myself and achieve the career success I have been blessed to experience. *Each of these opportunities represents an example to follow for leaders today.* In each case, my future boss personally interviewed me, got to know me, clearly laid out the opportunity with their company, and offered me a chance to make the most of it. Outside of a market-competitive pay package, they offered me nothing else except the promise of achievable *opportunity* if I was committed, worked hard, and produced results.

I wonder how seriously leaders take their critical role in the interview process today. I have witnessed an increased tendency for leaders to delegate this function exclusively to the HR and talent department, with the hiring manager being only marginally involved with the interview process. I know there are exceptions, but I challenge leaders today to get more involved in bringing the right talent into your companies. Partner closely with your HR and talent teams and make it clear you wish to be very involved in bringing on key hires. Make time for this vital function and let your future team members hear from your lips what they can expect from you and the company, clear details about opportunities to excel, and what *you* expect from *them*.

Beyond the Interview

Being more actively involved in the hiring process for key employees is only part of the equation. How will you continue to offer opportunities for growth and learning throughout a team member's career? I wrote a chapter in my 2022 book, *Upon Reflection*, about the need for leaders to always *ask*, *listen*, and *invest*. Staying close to your people this way will help you identify what they want to achieve in their careers. This will help you identify appropriate challenges to help them grow, and this in turn will enhance your ability to help them stay motivated and resist the temptation to leave for greener pastures.

Leaders, I encourage you to clearly identify the exciting opportunities you and your company have available for future and current team members. Get more involved in personally communicating this to potential key hires during the recruiting and interview process—and don't forget to include the current team. Take a more active role in asking, listening, and investing with your employees. Give them more opportunities to excel and grow while placing less emphasis on the excessive benefits and perks that may be getting out of hand. Coach the people leaders who may report to you to bring this emphasis on better communicating the company's opportunities to their teams as well and hold these leaders accountable for making this a priority.

Reflect a few months after you commit to this effort and assess the kinds of people this attracts to your team and the performance of the existing team. You will likely be pleasantly surprised.

> *Reflect on your experiences from earlier in your career. Were your experiences with opportunity similar to mine or different? What do you think of this idea of promoting training and development, income growth, and advancement opportunities in return for hard work and commitment? Are you willing to shift your thinking in this direction?*

CHAPTER 12

A Timeless Approach to Addressing Workplace Disconnectedness

Connection is the energy that exists between people when they feel seen, heard, and valued.

BRENÉ BROWN, *THE GIFTS OF IMPERFECTION*

Three of the many things I admire about my father, Steve, are his consistent habit of complimenting good work, encouraging others, and sincerely sharing gratitude. He is now eighty-five, and over the course of his long life, I've witnessed countless times him telling people he encountered in his daily travels when they were doing a good job, also including specifics about what he observed that inspired him to offer his compliment.

He would often ask to speak with their manager when possible and let them know what a good job the employee was doing. He would always strive to offer a warm smile, be patient, and encourage people who may be new in their job or struggling in some way. His old-school comments of "You are doing just fine" or "Keep at it; I know you can do it" provided the kind of reassurance we rarely hear anymore. Finally, he has always been the most grateful guy I know. He never fails to

71

let people know how appreciative he is—from his old work colleagues before he retired to the checkout person at Publix or the team member at Chick-fil-A who sells him his coffee. Having observed my father in action over the years, I have seen with my own eyes the positive impact he has had on others through their smiles and heartfelt appreciation for his kind words.

As inspiring as it might be, this chapter is not the story of a kind older gentleman who has spent his adult life being a good human to the people he encounters each day. I share this brief observation about my father because what he does so effortlessly and authentically is a powerful and much-needed example for all of us in today's business world. I'm concerned that we are forgetting the timeless importance of my father's mindset and the need to positively interact with our work colleagues at all levels of the organization. I don't often observe consistent behavior like this from leaders and aspiring leaders. It certainly exists, but it seems sporadic at best.

The Great Disconnect

If you are reading this chapter, regardless of your job title or generation, you have been the "new person" at some point in your career. We all know what it's like to start a new job after college, be assigned to a new team, or switch jobs and join a different company. Maybe this was a great experience for you . . . maybe not. Under the best of circumstances, starting your professional career or entering a new company environment can be difficult to navigate for the first few years, and we all could use a helping hand. In today's U.S. workforce, all generations of employees (especially Generation Z) are feeling more disconnected than ever. According to a 2023 survey by Gallup, only 33 percent of U.S. employees felt engaged at work:

> Employees still feel more detached from—and less satisfied with—their organizations and are less likely to connect to the companies' mission and purpose or to feel someone cares about them as a person.[1]

What can leaders do? If you will indulge me, I would like to share a very simple take on the role of leader: The role of a leader is to coach, guide, and inspire others to do their best. That's it. This basic definition has guided me my entire career, and as much as I love to read books on leadership to expand my understanding of the subject, I keep coming back to this clear and basic take as my guiding light. Many leaders I encounter today may intellectually agree with me, but they often struggle to overcome these three obstacles:

1. **Prioritization.** Leaders are faced with a barrage of business issues each day. It's easy to get hyper-focused on broken processes, poor revenue numbers, launching the new product, etc. *But can any of these be improved or accomplished without good people doing great work?* An old boss of mine told me many years ago that

1 Jim Harter, "In New Workplace, U.S. Employee Engagement Stagnates," January 23, 2024, Gallup Workplace, https://www.gallup.com/workplace/608675/new-workplace-employee-engagement-stagnates.aspx#:~:text=In%20the%20latest%20reading%2C%20from,than%202020's%20high%20of%2036%25.

the number-one responsibility of a leader is to focus on "getting the people right"—that everything else follows in terms of importance. Where does engaging, inspiring, and developing your team members sit on your list of priorities each day?

2. **Time**. If we are struggling with prioritization, we are likely struggling with time. Most leaders I know are in often unproductive meetings the majority of the workday. If we want to change, we have to be intentional and willing to try new approaches to creating time and space on our calendars. When do we meet individually with each direct report? When do we conduct skip-level meetings with more junior team members? Do we create time for "managing by walking around" and showing up to visit our team members on the front lines? Are we sincerely seeking candid feedback on how we can be better leaders? Are we asking the right questions? Are we truly listening to their needs? Do they know we care? Are we investing in their development?

3. **An approach that works**. The bigger the organization, the bigger the challenge for leaders to have meaningful interactions with their team members. A senior executive leading a three-hundred-person organization will likely struggle to have frequent one-on-one meetings with every employee.

Here are a number of effective approaches I have observed from effective senior leaders to combat the disconnectedness and lack of engagement in their teams and companies:

- **Town halls.** Frequent use of town hall meeting formats with small groups and the whole organization on a quarterly basis. Don't over script the events and allow plenty of time for audience participation and Q&A.
- **Weekly communication.** Find your medium. Some of my clients do a weekly ninety-second video clip and others stick to an email format, but they are sure to personalize it, talk about key priorities, cast vision, and inspire. They find a way to be vulnerable, which is one of the most attractive traits of a leader.
- **Get your assistant to organize skip-level one-on-one meetings every month.** Perhaps you might set a goal of meeting five to ten people a month individually—from the newest employee to someone who reports to your directs. Ask questions and carefully listen in these conversations. Make it psychologically safe for them to be open with you. People feel valued when they feel heard. Share your appreciation for their efforts.
- **Host monthly lunches and coffee meetings with small groups.** This works well with team members you infrequently encounter, and it works with virtual teams as well.
- **Expect more from your direct reports.** Hold them accountable for the same activities you are trying to do yourself and for teaching *their* directs to do the same. Make this an ongoing topic of leadership team meetings and your individual meetings with your directs to encourage implementation and practice. The most effective and successful senior leaders I know enthusiastically embrace the roles of coach and mentor

for their teams, and they teach and encourage their direct reports to do the same.

It's easy to look at this problem of workplace disconnectedness and feel overwhelmed. The issue is complicated, and this brief chapter has barely scratched the surface on how we can move forward. Perhaps, though, we can make meaningful progress by simply *returning to the basics*. Maybe my father's lifelong practice of noticing and complimenting good work, patiently encouraging people who are new or struggling, and sharing his sincere gratitude with a warm smile are all the inspiration you and I need to make a positive difference each day in the lives of those we encounter at work and in our personal lives. My dad has always known something profound that today's leaders should more carefully consider: Team members want to be heard, they want to be encouraged, they want to know we care about them, they want to know what they do matters, and they want to be appreciated. Maybe, just maybe, my dad figured out long ago how to solve the problem of disconnectedness in the workplace.

Lesson learned . . . I hope we will all make the effort to emulate this approach in the days and weeks ahead.

Did the high employee disengagement score surprise you? How are you doing with the overcoming the three obstacles I shared in this chapter? Are you willing to implement my father's simple approach? Utilize the lessons of this chapter to engage differently with your team and other team members in the organization over the coming weeks and look for signs of increased engagement and connection.

CHAPTER 13

Six Best Practices for Being More Patient with Others

The practice of patience toward one another, the overlooking of one another's defects, and the bearing of one another's burdens is the most elementary condition of all human and social activity in the family, in the professions, and in society.

FR. LAWRENCE G. LOVASIK, *THE HIDDEN POWER OF KINDNESS*

I often think about the virtue of patience and the years I have spent trying to cultivate this habit I so admire and appreciate in others. I reflected again on this topic earlier this year after having a relevant conversation with a past coaching client. This busy senior leader in a large Atlanta-based company described his frustration and impatience with a number of people on his team and in his peer group. I listened carefully, then shared some hard-fought experience about being more patient with others from my own career and some observations of others who I think do this well.

Here is a summary of the advice I offered this leader . . .

Putting myself in the shoes of others and seeing the world through their eyes has always been an effective approach to cultivating patience in my life. When I feel impatient with others, I try and force myself to realize that there may be understandable reasons for whatever they are doing to trigger my impatience, and there is likely no malicious intent. I work hard at not responding in the moment, especially if I am frustrated or impatient, and I make a sincere effort to understand why they are saying or doing the thing that is evoking this response in me. I assure you that I am not always successful, but it's gotten easier as I get older.

This idea of better understanding others, walking in their shoes, and seeing the world through their eyes is all becoming countercultural in today's world. I work with business professionals every day who are dealing with ever-increasing levels of stress and anxiety, overscheduled workdays, little time for meaningful conversations and nurturing relationships, and neglect of their own self-care. Lack of patience with others is a likely fruit of these environments and approaches to work and life. If this topic is resonating and you want to improve your level of patience with others, here are six best practices to consider:

1. **Be present.** When engaging with work colleagues, friends, family, or others, put the iPhone away and completely focus on the person or people in front of you. Schedule adequate time for these conversations. When your thoughts are occupied by your next appointment or to-do item, your impatience rises and you are only thinking about the future, not those deserving of your full attention. If at all possible, have conversations in-person as reading facial expressions and listening to the tone of one another's voices

improves the quality of all dialogue. Virtual meetings, with the camera on, are an acceptable alternative if there is no other option.

2. **Be curious.** You have to ask questions to truly understand why people think a certain way or do what they do. Ask how they are doing at work and outside of work. Ask them to explain their reasoning on decisions. Ask them if they understand your expectations. Ask them if they need help and how you can better support them. *Curiosity activates greater understanding and reduces impatience.*

3. **Actively listen.** When we are struggling with patience, listening can be very difficult. If we are genuinely curious, it follows that we also need to be good listeners. We may be learning the all-important "whys" behind behaviors that are making us feel impatient with others. Be mindful to not listen only until it is your turn to speak, but listen to better understand.

4. **Practice a little self-reflection.** Look in the mirror . . . am I to blame for my lack of patience with others? Did I adequately train/develop my team member(s)? Have I created clear expectations on what I want? Have I communicated clearly? Have I offered help and support? Did I explain the rules? Am I modeling the behavior I wish to see in others? Am I stressed, anxious, or burned out, and is this why I am feeling impatient? Did I practice sincere curiosity to perhaps learn of a personal burden my colleague or team member is carrying on their shoulders? Wasn't I once in the same situation as the person in front of me?

5. **Sleep on it.** When feeling impatient with others, if possible, it's always a good idea to not respond right away. Take a little time, perhaps twenty-four hours, to carefully consider all angles of the situation. Allow yourself to gain a sense of calm and peace. Word to the wise: Responding when impatient, frustrated, or angry is *never* a good idea. Also, avoid responding when feeling impatient via email or text (see best practice #1). I have learned over the years the tremendous benefits of this best practice.

6. **"Do unto others . . ."** The Golden Rule is an obvious and critical best practice for us to follow. We should be motivated to be more patient with others because we all need others to be patient with us. Reflect for a moment on how you've personally benefited from someone being patient with you. How did you feel? Did you thank them? Let these positive experiences in your life inform and motivate your own practice of patience with the people you encounter each day.

I often write about the importance of being good humans. Practicing patience with others helps us become more understanding, compassionate, empathetic, and fosters stronger relationships. Patience is an act of kindness. Our patience is a wonderful gift we can give to others.

The people I admire and respect most in my personal and professional life are all incredibly patient. I am always a work in progress and have a number of areas I wish to improve, but perhaps in the coming days I will simply focus on more intentionally practicing the virtue of patience. I hope this effort inspires others to do the same—and I pray they will also be more patient with me.

> *After reading this chapter, how would you assess your ability to be patient? Have you tried putting yourself in the shoes of others to better understand their behavior and motivations? Identify one person toward whom you are currently feeling impatience. Using the best practices in this chapter, work on showing them (and others who trigger you) more patience in the coming weeks.*

CHAPTER 14

Moving the Needle on Accountability

The ancient Romans had a tradition: Whenever one of their engineers constructed an arch, as the capstone was hoisted into place, the engineer assumed accountability for his work in the most profound way possible: He stood under the arch.

MICHAEL ARMSTRONG, FORMER CEO AND CHAIRMAN OF AT&T

In Chapter 8, we discussed an effective approach for leaders to have more impact in accountability conversations with individual members of their team. Let's think bigger. A common and pervasive challenge with leaders I encounter each week is their frustration with the lack of consistent accountability from their teams, boundary partners, and often the company as a whole. We acknowledge it's a problem, but we typically struggle to address it in practical and meaningful ways. Maybe there's a great book out there with all the answers . . . a quick Amazon search for books on this topic yielded more than *thirty-thousand* results! That feels a little overwhelming, and it can be difficult to even know where to begin. Perhaps we should start by keeping it simple and practical.

How do we define accountability? Accountability for a team member means accomplishing the things you said you would do. It's about taking personal responsibility for your work. It's also about trusting in your teammates, holding one another accountable, and knowing you can count on one another to get things done. A leader has the same responsibility as their team members, but also must *hold others accountable*. When a leader tolerates missed deadlines and incomplete work on a regular basis, these behaviors become the norm for the team. This lack of accountability has a ripple effect that negatively impacts performance and morale on the team.

What are the obstacles to improving accountability? In my experience, one of the most significant obstacles to improving accountability is *status quo thinking*, or doing something because that's the "way we have always done it." Many of the issues I would associate with lack of accountability come from "normalized defects"—negative behaviors or mindsets we acknowledge sometimes exist in our companies but are allowed to remain: lack of candor, lack of trust, dysfunctional business meetings, unclear communication, groupthink, confusing strategy, fear of failure, lack of role clarity, etc.

Another significant obstacle is our tendency to overcomplicate our thinking about accountability. It's clear from my brief Amazon book search that there are countless ideas out there to combat the problem. Teams and entire organizations can have systemic accountability issues that may require grander approaches, but the leaders I know who want to address this are looking for helpful and easy-to-use best practices they can implement now.

I would like to offer you an approach called the **Practical**

Accountability Formula that is practical, simple, and clear. Mastering and consistently implementing this formula will yield immediate results. To be effective, it will require self-awareness, self-discipline, and a willingness to change old habits.

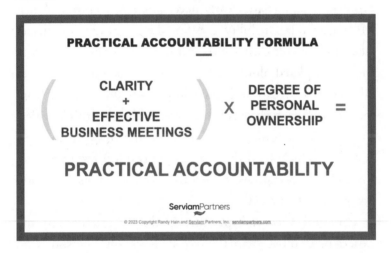

Clarity. It's a leader's responsibility to communicate and lead with clarity at all times. Leaders should always be clarifying the *why, who, what*, and *when* in every aspect of their daily work. Leaders should help clarify the roles and responsibilities of their team members. They should hold teams accountable to specific deadlines for work to be completed and clearly communicate the positive and negative consequences for making or missing these deadlines. Vagueness and ambiguity lead to confusion and ineffective results. *Good leadership creates clarity, not confusion.* Also, remember that clarity is not only the responsibility of senior executives. Each of us has a responsibility to model clarity, regardless of our role or title.

Effective Business Meetings. Unnecessary and unproductive business meetings are a common problem in most companies, and this contributes directly to challenges with *accountability* and *wasted time*. These ineffective meetings often take up time that could be better utilized for more important work. Some business meetings are clearly necessary, *but we can do better.* Missing agendas, inability to define the tasks to be completed, lack of clear task ownership, and unclear deadlines for work to be completed along with a failure to assign someone to take notes to recap and share important information from meetings are at the heart of this issue. Addressing this is critical to improving accountability as business meetings are the most common vehicle (and the easiest opportunity) for a leader to share clear expectations, review the work to be discussed and assigned, and set deadlines.

Personal Ownership. This is the "X factor." In my experience, most teams have at least one person who naturally and consistently takes ownership when needed and is willing to be held accountable for results. Most leaders likely achieved their positions partly because of a consistent ability to do this well. How about other team members who are reluctant to step up and accept responsibility or place their names next to tasks and projects with clear deadlines? What keeps them from showing more ownership? Is it fear? Lack of commitment? Trust issues? It's the job of a leader to understand why and the job of team members to embrace the importance of stepping up. Improving personal ownership for team members is both a *self-development opportunity* for them and an excellent *coaching opportunity* for their leaders. You can have amazing clarity and the world's most effective business meetings, but overall accountability for results will thrive, move slowly, or potentially fail based on the degree of personal ownership exhibited by each team member. I am reminded of the advice I received early in my career from a wise mentor: "If you touch it, you own it. Even if you only have 1 percent of the actual issue, act as if you have 100 percent. If we all act this way, our work will get done faster and our problems will quickly be solved." When used with discernment, a collaborative mindset, and good judgment, this is invaluable advice.

Each of these components of the Practical Accountability Formula is dependent on the other components and exist on a continuum. For example, if you rated your leadership clarity as an 8 out of 10, the effectiveness of your business meetings as 7 out of 10, and personal ownership from the team as 7 out of 10, you would generally have solid overall accountability for results from the team. In comparison, lower scores in each area *negatively* impact accountability. It is interesting to note that if there is zero personal ownership from the team, this results in zero accountability as anything x zero = zero. That's why I described it as the "X factor" earlier in the chapter and a true coaching opportunity for leaders to drive improvement.

It's also important to note that if we follow the simple definition at the beginning of the chapter, we have a shared accountability with one another on the team, not just accountability for our individual tasks. Our willingness to be held accountable and do our jobs well directly impacts every other member of the team, the team's overall performance, and that of the company. Accountability is both an individual goal and a commitment to our colleagues.

I hope you are willing to embrace this practical and simple approach as a way to begin moving the needle on accountability. The leaders and teams I know who follow it have experienced great results. If you are a leader at any level of your organization, here are some helpful steps to help you implement the Practical Accountability Formula at your next team meeting:

- **Create and share in advance an agenda that clearly spells out the purpose of the meeting, what you will discuss, and the deliverables and commitments you wish to see at the end of the meeting.** Send any pre-reads or requests for any work to be done in advance of the meeting to make sure everyone is well-prepared. *Make it clear that accountability with clear ownership and real deadlines for solutions are the goals for the meeting.*

- **Remind everyone at the beginning of the meeting that this is a psychologically safe place and ask everyone to be respectfully candid.** Also, make it clear that silence equals consent and this meeting is the best opportunity to voice opinions.

- **Ask someone to be the scribe for the meeting.** They should take notes on what is discussed, with an emphasis on writing a recap of the issue discussion and identifying who owns the solutions and their deadlines. *These notes should go out to all participants within twenty-four hours after the meeting.*

- **Identify and reach consensus on the problem to be addressed.** Be able to clearly identify why it is a problem, why this team is responsible for solving it, and the consequences to the business if it is not solved. Have some time allotted (twenty to thirty minutes) for discussing the issues to make sure everyone understands and is on board with what needs to be done.

- **Ask for volunteers to take ownership** for solving the issue or elements of the issue based on size or complexity. If nobody volunteers, assign someone you think is the best person to tackle the issue or task.
- **Ask each person given task ownership for a firm date commitment** on when they expect to have the task completed or the issue solved.
- **End the meeting with a clear understanding of the issue, who in the room owns solutions or pieces of the overall solution, and exactly when the work is to be done.** *The scribe should have all this captured in the notes/recap that goes out to everyone.*

If your bonus or compensation plans allow for this, one way to drive greater accountability is to share that team members who hit their metrics/goals *and* consistently take ownership and show accountability for getting results in these kinds of team discussions will have a greater chance of hitting or exceeding their bonus potential. Share that what each team member does with ownership and accountability will be an ongoing part of all quarterly performance reviews.

The leaders I know who excel at driving accountability are positive, motivational, and inspirational in their approach with the team. It is of vital importance for improving accountability that leaders raise their expectations regarding commitments on deliverables from their teams without over-indexing on negative consequences. Find an approach that works for you. Be consistent and fair with how you apply this with the team.

If you are ready to stop talking about accountability and start making real progress, this chapter was written for you, and I hope you find it helpful.

You can consider the lessons of this chapter as either a team member or the leader of a team. How do you show up in each of the three components of the Practical Accountability Formula? Rate yourself in each area and make a plan to improve over the coming weeks. Ask a teammate to help hold you accountable for progress.

CHAPTER 15

Thoughts on Repairing Your Personal Brand

It takes many good deeds to build a good reputation and only one bad one to lose it.

BENJAMIN FRANKLIN

Have you ever had a problem with your personal brand at work? Here is a true and somewhat genericized story (and a very common tale) I am sharing with permission. I was talking to a senior leader not long ago about struggles he was having with a lingering personal brand issue in a company he joined about a year ago. He had gone through a very stressful period the previous year with difficult personal challenges, a heavy travel schedule, long work hours, and a chaotic environment in his company, which was going through a significant reorganization. He shared, with some embarrassment, that he had been occasionally curt and ill-tempered with his team and peers during the worst two months of this period and had little interest or room on his calendar for investing in business relationships or developing his people. I have known this leader for over a decade, and the behavior he described was *very* uncharacteristic for him.

He has always been an empathetic and patient leader, easily accessible, with a passion for fostering good relationships and helping his work colleagues thrive. I would describe this as a blip in an otherwise successful career.

Eventually, the personal challenges he faced significantly changed for the better, his travel became less burdensome, and the schedule was more manageable. The company's reorganization was completed, and things began to return to normal . . . or so he thought. During his year-end review, his boss told him he heard there were problems with his personal brand. He shared that there was significant "talk" in the organization that he was not fully engaged, not available to his people or peers, and even had been verbally abusive to a few of them. His boss shared that some people assumed he was looking for another job. The leader owned his behavior during this stressful period, but he told his boss the issues being shared had become exaggerated and a little blown out of proportion. He shared that he had apologized to his team and peers after the difficult time, but he also recognized he obviously did not do enough as people were still frustrated and discussing it among themselves. He felt he had returned over the last few months to being the type of leader he had always been, but he committed to his boss that he would take the conversation to heart, own and address necessary changes, and work on repairing his brand. In addition to the frustration with his own struggles and subsequent uncharacteristic behavior, the leader shared with me that he was hurt that nobody on his team or peers had approached him with this candid feedback and lingering concerns.

Knowing I am an executive coach, he asked for my counsel

on what he should do. He also wanted my advice on ensuring it never happened again. This is typically the perfect situation to partner with an executive coach and go through a robust 360 interview process, do assessment testing, and develop a specific development plan to help navigate a way forward. Because of his company's current financial state, they were not able to make this financial investment in him. The advice I share in the rest of this chapter is a combination of approaches I encouraged this leader to take over our breakfast meeting, but it's also advice *for all of us*. I would suggest that at times, we may be the leader in this story and struggle with some sort of personal brand issue. We also may be at times the colleagues around this leader who miss an opportunity to give candid feedback, make incorrect assumptions, fail to ask questions and learn the "why" behind behaviors, contribute to gossip, and miss opportunities to help a colleague going through a difficult time.

Advice for This Leader (and Anyone Who Has Dealt with a Similar Challenge)

As he and I reflected on the roots of his brand issue, I pointed out the obvious—that he had been under enormous stress on the personal and business fronts. Managing stress well at every level of your career is critical because if neglected, prolonged stress can often bring out behaviors that are the *opposite* of our normal behaviors, and we may not even be aware of it. He acknowledged that he saw the signs but did very little to proactively manage his stress. Instead he felt he was just trying to survive.

What steps could he have taken then and also adopt for the future?

- **Don't suffer in silence.** I gently pointed out that he should have had the courage to confide in his boss that he needed help and ask for a little less travel, grace around his personal issues, and accountability from his leader if there were any concerns about how he was showing up and engaging with others. He has a good relationship with his boss and will not hesitate to do this in the future.
- **Manage stress through exercise, prayer, meditation, or whatever works for you.** This leader has always been very fit, but he neglected his exercise routines and never thought to seek help through prayer or any other means during the height of his stress.
- **Seek help.** Unchecked stress can be a killer with severe negative impacts to your brain and body. Sometimes you may need the advice of your physician or the guiding hand of a professional therapist to help you navigate through periods of high stress.

We discussed a few other approaches that would have been very helpful during and after this period of difficulty:

- **Be vulnerable.** He, like many leaders I know, was uncomfortable with being vulnerable. What would have happened if he had shared with trusted peers and team members a little of what he was facing at home and work? Discernment and good judgement are important. He didn't need to share *everything*, but letting people know he would be grateful for their patience, help, and grace until things settled down in his life would have very likely created an environment of understanding and helped him avoid some of the brand issues that emerged. Chapter 16 will help you go much deeper on this topic.

- **Provide psychological safety and consistently ask for specific, candid feedback.** Did his colleagues feel safe giving him candid feedback? Why were there lingering brand issues? What was keeping people from coming directly to him with their thoughts and concerns? In my professional experience, the fear of giving candid feedback at work is pervasive. One helpful approach is to *give others permission to be candid with you.* It's also important to always provide psychological safety when asking for candid feedback from colleagues, especially more junior members on the team. They need to know there will be no repercussions for speaking with candor. Also, seeking candid feedback has to be more than simply asking "Is everything okay?" We should be specific when we ask for feedback. Examples might look like:
  - "What are two or three things you would like to see me do differently in how I lead the team?"
  - "Are you getting what you need from me as a colleague or a leader? What are a few areas where I can do more and improve?"
  - "I recognize I have not been myself the last few months and I sincerely apologize. What are some specific behaviors of mine you have observed of late you think I can improve?"

The bottom line is that people need to feel safe speaking up, and they need to be asked questions that will generate specific responses you can use, not just the usual generic answers. Helpful tip: Don't be defensive and always be grateful for the feedback!

- **Cultivate accountability partners.** Whom can we count on to tell us the truth? Who will pull us aside when we get off track and help us correct our course? Mistakenly, this leader looked back, assuming that someone should have stepped up and held him accountable for his behavior, but nobody did. Even his boss waited until the year-end review to give feedback. This may speak to the surface nature of his relationships in this company he has worked at for less than a year or a lack of vulnerability because others may have felt he didn't need or want their help. *Accountability partner relationships need to be intentionally cultivated and treasured.* We all need at least one trusted person who always has permission to kick us in the rear end if we need it.

Advice for the Rest of Us

Similar to how we used to dissect the characters in a story during our college literature classes, let's imagine we are the team members around this leader with the damaged brand. I hope we can agree that the leader must own his behavior, but should things have gone on as long as they did? Did he need to wait until his year-end review to be challenged by his boss and learn there were lingering issues? While he has plenty to think about regarding lessons learned and how he can avoid this problem in the future, we might consider for ourselves whether we have contributed (or are contributing) in an unhealthy way to issues like this in our workplaces.

Below are five key behaviors we all might reflect on and adopt in order to positively help our colleagues who may be going through similar brand challenges:

1. **Avoid assumptions.** How often do we find ourselves making assumptions about our colleagues? We observe a behavior or hear a comment and think we have a person pegged—that we know everything about them. Assumptions are dangerous as they can often be the catalyst for derailing somebody's career and poor business decisions.

2. **Implement the "No Gossip Rule."** Let's have the professional maturity to never discuss a colleague if they are not present in the room with us. Gossip, often fueled by poor assumptions, spreads like wildfire and does great damage to personal brands inside a company. If we won't say what we think to the person's face, let's not say it all. Instead of "What is _____'s problem?" let's focus on "_____, how can I help you?"

3. **Be more curious.** The antidote to assumption is curiosity. Rather than guess or speculate, ask questions. If we observe bad behavior or experience a person in a way that's not typical, let's be more curious. "Are you doing OK? You seem out of sorts and a bit stressed. Is there anything I can do to help?" Curiosity opens doors, expands our understanding, leads to solutions, and is always the right path to follow.

4. **Give grace.** Could any of us get through a week without a little grace thrown our way? There is always somebody, often unknown to us, overlooking our worst behavior, tolerating our mistakes, giving us the benefit of the doubt, and willing to help us get back on track. Grace is comprised of patience, understanding, forgiveness, and love. I would wager we all like to receive it, but maybe we all could all do a better job of giving it to our colleagues when they get off track.

5. **Sincerely offer to help.** This may seem obvious, but in my experience, I don't see it often enough. When someone at work is struggling and we have practiced the preceding four behaviors well, the natural next step is to help, coach, mentor, and advise our colleague in addressing their issues. Be respectfully candid, give concrete examples of the behavior you observed, and offer helpful solutions.

I don't think I have ever encountered another professional (including myself) who didn't deal with a negative personal brand issue at least once in their career. If you are in this situation, follow the steps above I shared with the leader over breakfast as a starting point. We have a responsibility to address these issues for ourselves, but we also have an obligation to help our colleagues when they are going through the same thing. It is simply the right thing to do, and remember, the struggling colleague may one day be *us*.

THOUGHTS ON REPAIRING YOUR PERSONAL BRAND

Have you experienced negativity around your personal brand? How did you deal with it? Have you worked with a colleague experiencing this challenge? Is someone you know dealing with this now? I encourage you to practice the five behaviors I shared as the most effective approach for getting your co-worker back on track.

CHAPTER 16

Turning Our Vulnerabilities into Something Positive

A leader, first and foremost, is human. Only when we have the strength to show our vulnerability can we truly lead.

SIMON SINEK

If you are reading this chapter, you are human. You are imperfect, just like me and everyone else you know. I hope you will embrace the obvious truth of this but also recognize how most of us are fearful of letting people see our flaws and imperfections . . . even though we know (and everyone else knows) we have them.

Why is it so difficult to be vulnerable?

A few clear obstacles to vulnerability I have observed include fear of being judged, concern our vulnerability will be used against us, and having the right words to use when sharing our vulnerability. We may also incorrectly assume that being vulnerable usually involves sharing deeply personal and emotional areas of our lives, instead of recognizing that *asking for help, saying we don't know the answer,* or *owning a mistake* are also appropriate forms of vulnerability. Perhaps we should consider viewing vulnerabilities as existing on a spectrum from one to one hundred, with more comfortable forms of vulnerability existing near the lower end and more uncomfortable manifestations of it living near the higher end.

As I reflected on this topic, I came to the realization that the people I am closest to and most admire are all exceptional at being vulnerable. These individuals are relatable, accessible, and trustworthy—and most of my best relationships exist within this special group. They routinely transform what many may see as their liabilities and challenges into positive strengths that inspire, motivate, and help others. How do they do it? What sets them apart?

Here are five helpful approaches for turning vulnerabilities into strengths:

1. **Use discernment and good judgment.** The appropriate sharing of vulnerability is guided by the use of *discernment* and *good judgment*. Always read the room, know your audience, and consider the timing of your words. Be mindful to not overshare. Sharing should always be considered a good thing, but sometimes we need to get to know someone over time before sharing really personal things. Consider sharing individually instead of with a group. Pick your moments and audience well.

2. **Vulnerability is critical for relationship-building.** Do you have any great relationships where some level of sharing vulnerabilities does not exist? Likely not. We should all be motivated to build thriving relationships inside and outside of work; the mutual sharing of weaknesses, flaws, and challenges actually draws us to other people. Our vulnerability invites others to be vulnerable. As C.S.

Lewis said in *The Four Loves*, "Friendship is born at that moment when one person says to another: 'What! You too? I thought I was the only one.'"

3. **Tell inspiring stories.** The stories that inspire me most are not always about triumphs and successes, but about overcoming struggles, dealing with adversity, or even lessons learned from failure. I often write about my oldest son who has autism. I share his story because I am very proud of how he navigates the difficulties of everyday life and inspires everyone who knows him. Sometimes our toughest challenges, as difficult as they may be to endure, can provide hope and inspiration for others if we are willing to share.

4. **Seek teachable moments.** The best leaders I know are vulnerable leaders. Why? They consistently seek out *teachable moments* for their colleagues and harness the power of vulnerability to make those moments memorable. For example, I worked with a client some years ago who was insatiably curious, an exceptional listener, and strong developer of her people. She always wanted to see how her team was doing, where they needed help, and how they were growing. Her "secret sauce" in those conversations was her willingness to share with the team moments of struggle and failure from her own career. She was relatable and believable to those around her, which let them know she understood their issues, and her helpful coaching was often the fruit of her rich experiences.

5. **Humility activates vulnerability.** It is almost impossible to truly be vulnerable without being humble. The

humility of admitting we are human, imperfect, and make mistakes activates the practice of vulnerability. In the words of Patrick Lencioni, "The key to being vulnerable is humility. People who cannot come to terms with the truth about themselves—and truth is the essence of humility—will not be comfortable with vulnerability."

Sometimes, the practice of vulnerability requires patience and grace. I was not very vulnerable early in my career, but getting married, having children, growing in my faith, experiencing the challenges of life, and the simple passage of time have helped me grow considerably in this area. I have learned to be patient and give myself grace just as others have extended these same gifts to me.

From my own experience, I would suggest that our ability to flourish personally and professionally is interlinked with the appropriate practice of vulnerability. If you reflect on this chapter and feel you are not as vulnerable as you could or should be, be patient with yourself and do what works for you. Take a few baby steps. Practice being more vulnerable with people you trust. Ask for help and accountability from a few key people in your life. Let's get started.

Reflect on your own willingness to be vulnerable. Is this a challenge? What holds you back? If you seek to improve in this area, practice the five approaches shared in this chapter. Work on being more appropriately vulnerable with at least two people over the next two weeks. Gauge both how you feel and also how they are responding to you.

CHAPTER 17

A Road Map for Effectively Serving on Nonprofit Boards

We make a living by what we get,
but we make a life by what we give.
WINSTON CHURCHILL

I challenge all leaders, at every stage of their careers, to be *servant leaders* . . . seeking opportunities to selflessly share their time, talent, and treasure with their communities and worthy causes. During the course of my thirty-plus years in business, I have had the good fortune to serve both as a volunteer for various causes and on a number of nonprofit boards. I am grateful for the enriching experiences, the amazing people I have met, and the wonderful causes I have been privileged to serve. One of the benefits I've gleaned from years of community service is the knowledge of how to effectively serve on a nonprofit board. This chapter seeks to summarize the lessons I've gleaned into an easy-to-follow road map that will hopefully enrich your nonprofit board service experience and help add value to the organizations you serve.

"Why should I serve on *this* nonprofit board?" is the fundamental question we should ask ourselves before accepting a board position. Our time is often stretched thin, and free minutes are precious, so evaluate any extra time commitments with thoughtful discernment. I recommend asking the following questions as part of the evaluation process:

- What is the reputation of the organization in the community? Is the leadership team effective? Can I speak with references and existing board members?
- How often does the board meet and what is the time commitment required of board members?
- Does the board have D&O (Directors and Officers) insurance?
- What will I have to sacrifice personally and professionally in order to give this organization what it requires of me?
- Can I involve my family and friends in the activities of the organization?
- Do my passions, values, and interests align with the mission of the organization?
- Will my skills and experiences help me be effective on the board?
- Am I willing to champion the cause of this organization to my network and potentially ask for donations?
- Is there a minimum personal donation required of board members?

In my first board member role more than twenty-five years ago, I was so excited to be invited that I didn't ask many questions. Even though the mission of the organization aligned with my passions and interests, I quickly learned that the nonprofit had a dysfunctional leadership team, a poor reputation in the community, and a desperate need for me to help them raise money. It was a painful lesson for me, but I learned from it.

Let's be honest here. Ask yourself if your desire to serve on a nonprofit board is to truly make a difference or a way to build your resume. I have worked alongside professionals from both camps. The people who have a heart for service add significant value and find their experience rewarding. People wanting to serve for the sake of appearances can have a negative effect on the organization by not contributing at the expected level and taking the seat of someone who is willing to be more active.

Innovative Ways to Add Value

Did you know there are other ways to help the organizations you are serving besides writing a big check? While individual contributions are obviously helpful and needed, we may not always be in a position to provide significant financial resources. I have helped develop alternative ways to provide value to the nonprofits I have served. Here are a few proven ideas:

- **The small gathering.** Host a small, intimate gathering (ten to fifteen people) in your office or at a local restaurant where other business leaders can hear a guest speaker present on a relevant topic. This can be an author, recognized business leader, or a professional service provider offering their views on a relevant business topic or market trends. Invite the head of your nonprofit organization and make introductions. Provide a meal in a relaxed setting and invite people who have a heart for giving back. This approach creates more awareness in the business community for the nonprofit, attracts potential volunteers for the organization's projects, and draws potential donors.

- **The Leadership Forum concept.** This is a modification of the above idea, but requires you to think bigger. Three times a year, my firm hosts a Leadership Forum at one of the ROAM Innovative Workplace locations (www.meetatroam.com). We invite seventy-five to one hundred senior business leaders to hear someone of interest present on a relevant business topic. We often select a nonprofit I know as a "Community Sponsor," place their logo and information in our marketing materials, and recognize them at the Forum. We invite the organization's leader to say a few words and offer a place for them to distribute marketing information. The events are free, and we invest in coffee and a light breakfast for the attendees. Everyone involved—the speaker, attendees, hosting firms, and the nonprofit—benefits.

- **Gifts that matter.** Every Christmas, many of us give generously to our clients and business colleagues to whom we wish to show our appreciation. Next year, instead of giving the overstuffed gift basket or box of cookies, make a donation on their behalf to your favorite nonprofit. Each year my firm makes donations to worthy causes in the name of clients and friends; the response has been wonderful, and we are able to help in a meaningful way the causes we support throughout the year.

- **Open your network.** Actively introduce key business leaders and other valuable resources to the leaders of the nonprofits you serve. If you are aware of its organizational needs, you may be able to get friends to donate their skills and professional services pro bono, which is of enormous value. This can also be a useful way to help recruit additional board members. The coffee and lunch meetings you facilitate can often produce a lot of positive results for both parties, and it's as simple as sending an introductory email.

- **Promote, promote, promote.** Use email and social media to promote the nonprofits you serve. LinkedIn, Facebook, and Twitter (X) updates on upcoming events for your nonprofits can help raise their profile in the community. Send updates to your network when the organization is in the news or if any of the leadership is quoted. This is incredibly valuable and costs a minimal investment of time.

Things to Avoid

As much as this chapter is about things to do, I also want to address what to avoid when serving on a nonprofit board. Here are a few observations from my experiences about what NOT to do:

- **Don't overcommit.** Be prudent with your time when volunteering for a board or committee assignment. I only serve on boards that align with my top three passions. This keeps me focused and allows me to add true value to my favorite causes.

- **Don't be impatient.** Nonprofits typically don't run like our companies, and process, deadlines, and growing revenue can often be alien concepts.
- **Don't forget to "experience" what the nonprofit is all about.** Don't serve on a board and fail to get personally involved in their mission. Get out in the field and help! You can't sell what you haven't experienced firsthand.
- **Don't ignore the need to build collaborative friendships on the board.** You will be relying on one another in the future to get things done, so spend quality time with your fellow board members. I'm grateful for the incredible friendships I have built through my years of board service.
- Don't be ungrateful. Here is a helpful tip a mentor gave me two decades ago that I have never forgotten: "Don't ever serve on the board of a nonprofit and expect them to be grateful to you. That is absolutely the wrong attitude. You should always be grateful for the opportunity to serve their worthy cause."
- **Don't overstay your welcome.** You should never look at any board service as a "life sentence." Serve with passion and help the organization to the best of your ability, but always be developing your replacement to give others the same opportunity to serve that you have been given. You can still support the organization after you exit the board, but I would recommend not serving on a board beyond a two- or three-year term.

I am a better person because I give time to serve nonprofits in my community. As I have gotten older, I'm keenly aware of what causes I am passionate about and what I truly have to offer. My hope is that the thoughts in this chapter will stimulate deeper thinking about where you can make a difference, help maximize your own nonprofit board experiences, and make a more meaningful contribution in the community. Even if you are not ready or able to serve on a board, nonprofits always need volunteers, and that might be a great place to begin.

We have much to offer, these organizations need our help, and much good can come from our efforts.

Have you served (or are you currently serving) on a nonprofit board? Reflect on your experiences. Having read this chapter, how will you engage differently going forward? If you are considering serving on a board in the future, utilize these best practices to maximize your experience.

CHAPTER 18

Aspirational Priorities versus Actual Priorities

The price of anything is the amount of life you exchange for it.
HENRY DAVID THOREAU

If you and I were to have a calm conversation about priorities away from the hustle and bustle of the daily work environment, we would likely list the usual suspects. For me, my top priorities (in this order) are faith, family, health, and work. You may have a similar list that accurately captures what matters most to you. These *aspirational* priorities sound good and feel good, and we genuinely wish to honor them, but they often enter into brutal conflict each week with the challenging demands of our jobs. We often wind up giving the important priorities outside of work the scraps of time left over from our busy workdays. On the aspirational priority list, work may be last. On the actual priority list, *work is often the top priority*.

I would suggest that the practical way to address this critical issue is considering how to improve our self-discipline and embrace intentionality. We likely know what we need and want to do, but we may struggle to get it all done. Perhaps one of the best places to start is considering where we spend our time and developing useful routines. Let me give you an example.

For many years, I have been intentional about finding time for and preparing at the beginning of each day to be at the top of my game for clients, friends, and family. I have been an early riser since childhood, and my early morning ritual has been consistent for the last few decades. While some people like to exercise early in the day, I prefer to work out at lunch or late in the afternoon as a form of stress release and instead use my early morning time for prayer, reflection, reading, and creative writing.

I wake up at 4:45 a.m. every day and enjoy the first of my two cups of coffee. I say a prayer and do some spiritual or business reading, always looking to feed and expand my mind. I have a healthy breakfast, enjoy a second cup of coffee and do some writing, usually a blog post or a chapter for a future book. I sometimes work on creating new leadership development content for my business. Around 6:15 a.m., I check on the news of the day, send a few emails, manage administrative aspects of my business, and prepare for my first meeting, which is typically at 7:00 or 7:30 a.m. Monday through Friday. I follow a similar routine on the weekends— without the early meetings and emails, of course.

This focused routine prepares me to fully engage with the leaders I work with and be an alert and active listener and coach attuned to their needs. I feel sharp, creative, and focused, and I credit this intentional and disciplined approach to starting the day for allowing me to give the best of myself to others. I'm grateful that my business has thrived over the years, in part because of this morning ritual and the impact it has on my day.

Two of the keys to improving self-discipline, mastering intentionality, and developing routines is *practicing self-awareness* and *learning how to say no.* For example, I have known most of my life that I am naturally sharpest and have the most energy in the morning. As a high-functioning introvert, I also know I'm at my best engaging with others from 7:00 a.m. to around 4:00 p.m. most days. I am typically scheduled with individual clients or leadership teams the vast majority of each day Monday through Friday.

Because high-functioning introverts and introverts tend to run out of energy for people by mid to late afternoon, I carve out thirty to forty minutes for exercise (usually intense cardio) between 11:00 a.m. and 1:00 p.m. every day, and I also take a two-mile walk (weather permitting) at the end of the workday before having dinner with my family. These exercise windows allow me to relieve stress, help restore some of my energy for people, and contribute significantly to my overall mental health and physical fitness.

The end-of-the-day walk is particularly important to me; I turn my phone off, engage in some prayer, and use the remaining walking time for deep thinking and reflection. I also have recently added a twenty- to thirty-minute window for reading after my walk, which has been very helpful. I'm then ready to fully engage with my family at dinner and be present for them the rest of the evening.

I am self-aware about my needs, but I have also worked hard for years at learning to effectively and respectfully say no. The exercise time on my calendar is the time slot I work hardest to protect. It has been a fixture on my calendar since early 2020, and I schedule all of my work around it. There are a few exceptions when I will move the exercise time, but they are rare. When I say no to someone who wants this protected time slot, I immediately offer alternative times and do my best to be helpful and accommodate their request when it will work for both our calendars.

Why does all this matter?

The leaders I admire and try to emulate wisely practice self-care and are intentional about taking care of their physical, emotional, spiritual, and mental needs. They understand (and I completely agree) that *you cannot share with others from an empty cup.*

One last helpful tip to promote better self-discipline, intentionality, and useful routines is to place every important personal and professional goal or to-do on the calendar each week. This may seem obvious, but in my experience most businesspeople *only* schedule the work-related items and fail to schedule the equally or more important personal stuff. The result is that the priorities and important areas of our personal lives only get the scraps of time left over from our hectic workdays. *Be more intentional.* Schedule everything important in your life (kid's activities, exercise, doctor visits, thinking time, prayer time, volunteering, anniversaries, birthdays, etc.) to ensure that nothing falls through the cracks. In my life, if something is on my calendar, it is highly likely to get done.

Working and living in the post-COVID age has affected all of us for better or worse. Although I greatly respect the severity of the pandemic and its impact on people's lives, I also am grateful for the forced positive changes in work habits and routines many of us have experienced. In the old days, I left my home early to meet with clients throughout the day and got home just in time for dinner. Today, I feel very fortunate to run my business with a hybrid approach that allows me to work with my global clients virtually and schedule local in-person meetings more selectively, which is currently about seven to ten times per week. My business is thriving, I feel healthy and fully engaged, my productivity is vastly improved, and my clients are well-served. I believe the hybrid work model is here to stay, and I embrace it.

I don't pretend to have all the answers, and I often struggle to do all of this well, but I keep trying to improve. Time is a precious resource, and we need to be good stewards of how we spend it. I believe greater intentionality, good routines, and better self-discipline are the keys to igniting more success in life and business. If we achieve progress in making this a reality, life and work will be richer and more enjoyable because of our efforts.

How does this idea of aspirational versus actual priorities speak to you? After reading this chapter, how will you think differently about work and life this week and beyond? What steps can you begin making to develop better self-discipline, be intentional, and adopt healthy routines? How can you reinforce what is already working for you? Consider finding an accountability partner so you can challenge each other to make improvements.

CHAPTER 19

Getting Off to a Great Start: Advice for Leaders in New Roles

Transitions are periods of opportunity, a chance to start afresh and to make needed changes in an organization. But they are also periods of acute vulnerability, because you lack established working relationships and a detailed understanding of your new role.

MICHAEL WATKINS, *THE FIRST 90 DAYS*

If you are reading this book, you will likely take on at least one new role before the end of your career (in some cases, a few new roles). How you get started in the new job makes all the difference. Onboarding for new leaders has been a relevant business topic and on the radar of most HR leaders inside larger organizations since the mid-nineties when *The First 90 Days* by author Michael Watkins was released. Many companies followed his challenge to create helpful onboarding experiences for their new hires, particularly in leadership roles. These experiences varied greatly and had mixed results. Some organizations defined onboarding as "employee orientation," while others left it to the new leaders to figure out for themselves, providing little or no organizational support.

In my capacity as an executive coach for senior executives,

I have long observed how critical the first few months are to a new leader's success. Because of the typically rapid pace of business and an increasing lack of focus on individual leader development, leaders in new roles are often left to navigate the first months on their own without an effective road map for success or a coach to guide them.

What is your situation? Perhaps you have performed well and received a well-earned promotion to a more senior position in your company. Maybe you were recruited from outside the organization into a leadership role. Once the excitement wears off, the serious work of getting off to a good start in your new job will require your full attention. *Are you prepared?*

Twelve Obstacles to Success for New Leaders

It can be difficult to anticipate all of the issues a newly promoted or hired leader might face in their first few months on the job. Here is a list of potential obstacles that can derail success in a new job based on my observations and experience:

1. **Making a poor first impression.** Transition can sometimes overwhelm and overload leaders. Keeping attention focused on what's most important, prudent decisions, and strong communication can help build positive first impressions.

2. **Getting promoted within the "family."** Leaders promoted from within an organization are often elevated to a leadership role over former peers. This can be a difficult adjustment period and should be addressed with humility, empathy, and a lot of open conversations. Some of your former peers will cheer you, and some

will be envious. Be grateful to the first group and work diligently to enlist the support of the second group.

3. **Go-it-alone syndrome.** A lack of willingness to ask for help and acting like you have all the answers works against the collaboration and teamwork you should be pursuing.

4. **Failure to be curious.** One of the best ways to break down walls and build rapport is to practice insatiable curiosity with your new circle of peers and colleagues. You will learn important information about people and the organization while demonstrating humility and a genuine interest in others.

5. **Being blinded by the spotlight.** All eyes are on you in the new position (or at least it sometimes feel that way). Don't let the glare of real or perceived attention detract from focusing on the fundamentals and establishing yourself in the new role.

6. **Becoming isolated.** The failure to quickly build relationships with new teammates and establish connections with key stakeholders can derail a leader as they look to exert influence or rally support for their ideas/projects down the road.

7. **Taking on too much.** Being a new leader can create anxiety about being perceived as a "doer" and lead to taking on too much work too soon. The overloaded leader is soon drowning and missing deadlines or goals, leading to a poor first impression.

8. **Falling behind the learning curve.** This often occurs when the new leader does not prepare effectively prior to the start date or in the early days on the job. This leads to a less-than-adequate understanding

of the situation, customers, key business partners, organizational capabilities, or market conditions, which can impede an effective transition.

9. **Failure to acclimate to the new culture.** A new leader must be willing to adapt to the new territory, learn new approaches, and embrace fresh strategies to remain effective. It's important to learn the way decisions are made and how to get things done. Seek to understand the "unwritten" rules of the organization and how to avoid the political traps.

10. **Sticking with an underperforming team too long or failing to deliver.** In many cases, new leaders are brought in because of performance issues. When new leaders give the existing team members too many chances, they risk losing credibility in the eyes of the stronger players. Failure to build a high-performing team and deliver results quickly can be difficult for a new leader to recover from. **Helpful tip:** Take the time to see who the best performers are on your team or who is capable of being developed before making significant people moves. Be careful to avoid a scorched earth approach before assessing who can contribute in meaningful ways to the team's success.

11. **Failure to chart a new course or develop a winning strategy.** Often, bold new ideas and a different strategy are needed sooner rather than later. Instead of delaying the needed changes too long, gather data and input from key stakeholders and boldly move forward if the circumstances merit this approach. Remember: new leaders are rarely placed in their positions to preserve the status quo.

12. **Swinging for the fences versus achieving small wins.** Often, a new leader desires to make a big splash and establish their reputation. This path is risky. Instead, go for small attainable wins in the first few weeks before attempting bolder moves.

Twelve Best Practices to Help New Leaders Get Off to a Good Start

Okay, so now you are in the new job and have a better understanding of the potential derailers to your success. What are proven ways to effectively manage your onboarding and get off to a good start? Here are twelve best practices to consider:

1. **Identify and cultivate relationships with key stakeholders.** Who has the most impact on your business and areas of responsibility? Develop a stakeholder map with the help of HR and your boss. Be intentional about getting to know these key stakeholders early on and build collaborative partnerships. Know who your internal and external customers are and how to serve them best. You will struggle later if this key step is overlooked.

2. **Cultivate candor.** Many companies struggle with the idea of candid conversations. Ambiguity, political correctness, and the absence of candor can be a drag on a company's culture and negatively impact business results. Candor should be modeled, encouraged, never punished, and always delivered with respect and professionalism. Show your team and peers how to do it!

3. **Partner with human resources.** Don't ignore this vital resource and the tools at their disposal as you evaluate

your team. Rely on HR early in the process and build a strong partnership moving forward. HR is not the enemy. They are the keepers of important people data you will require to be successful.

4. **Be humble and ask for help.** The dumb questions are the ones we never ask. Everyone has likely been in your shoes; so don't let pride prevent you from asking for help. If you avoid acting like you know everything on the first day, it will demonstrate humility and endear you quickly to your team and peers.

5. **Build broad relationships.** Don't just cultivate your new boss and peers—branch out and get to know leaders in all areas of the organization. Your effectiveness in the future may be impacted (positively or negatively) by your ability to draw on resources and relationships across the organization. Two coffees or lunches a week with new colleagues is a productive goal in your first three months; this will bear fruit down the road.

6. **Establish clear and candid communication with your new boss.** Within days of beginning your new role, establish expectations, goals, and preferred communication with your new boss. Can you both agree on what your success in the first year looks like? It is best to get on the same page quickly and cultivate candid rapport to maximize your likelihood of success. Also, be sure to ask for specific feedback on how you are doing.

7. **Set goals.** What is your thirty/sixty/ninety-day plan? What milestones do you plan to reach in the first three months? What goals do you have for your team during

this time frame and beyond? Are you in alignment with your boss? Establish and communicate these goals clearly and frequently.

8. **Assess your team.** Partner with HR to understand the talent you have inherited and the performance gaps on your team. Get input from peers and your boss. Don't delay this critical exercise or you will negatively impact your long-term effectiveness.

9. **Wisely manage expectations.** The old maxim "under-promise and over-deliver" is applicable to the early months in a new leadership position. Don't create unrealistic expectations. Wait until you have truly assessed the organization and the capabilities of your team before making bold public commitments.

10. **Listen, listen, listen.** Be a great listener before offering your insights on the challenges of the organization or better ways to get things done. Listen carefully to people who know more than you, offer insight when appropriate, and always be seen as someone who values good counsel.

11. **Be authentic.** We must challenge the fear that somehow being real is a bad thing. It may be uncomfortable, but practicing transparency, engaging in honest and open dialogue, and always placing your principles and ethics before advancing your career will bring you greater success in every aspect of your life.

12. **Make the most of the moment!** All eyes are on a new leader. There is a window of opportunity to seize in the first ninety days when a new leader commands a heightened degree of attention. Be prudent and

thoughtful, but make your mark and don't feel bound to emulate the approach of your predecessor (unless of course, that approach was working well!).

Taking on a new leadership role and leading a new team or organization is always a challenge—hopefully a positive one. My hope in sharing these onboarding obstacles and best practices is that you will avoid the pitfalls that I have seen affect so many leaders over the course of my career and get off to a positive and productive start. You may have landed the opportunity of a lifetime, so investing time and energy on the front end of your new venture should be a priority.

Always remember the importance of self-awareness. Take stock of how you are doing by seeking input from candid people in your circle who will tell you the truth, not merely what you wish to hear. Be intentional but also thoughtful in your actions. Balance decisiveness with prudent judgment.

Finally, remember you that you deserve to be here. Be confident, be authentic, draw on your past experiences, and enthusiastically embrace the challenges placed before you.

Reflect on when you have been promoted to (or hired into) a new role. Looking back, what would you do differently? How do these obstacles and best practices resonate with you? You have an opportunity to approach your own onboarding differently next time, and this chapter will help, but you also have an opportunity to utilize these best practices to help colleagues and new members who join your team.

CHAPTER 20

The 80/20 Rule and Better Listening

There is a difference between truly listening and waiting for your turn to talk.

RALPH WALDO EMERSON

I had a great conversation with my younger son a few years ago one Saturday as we ran errands and grabbed lunch on his last day of winter break before he headed back to college for his junior year. In the past when my son was much younger, I had a tendency to jump right into the topics I wished to discuss, saying things like "How was school today?" or "How did you do on your history quiz?" and the ever-annoying dad question: "What do you want to do with the rest of your life?"—you get the picture. His responses were typically "okay," "fine," or "I don't know." Sound familiar?

As my son entered his late teens, I worked harder to meet him where he was at. That particular Saturday's conversation was an example of this transition as we talked about sports, the books he was reading, his impressions on the events of the day, spring break plans, and a number of other topics that interested him. I tried to just ask topical questions and let him talk without interruption while I practiced *active listening*. At some point in the conversation, when he felt comfortable, we touched on weightier and more substantive issues like life after college, internships, friendships, faith, grades, etc. But this substantive part of the dialogue was at most only 20 percent of the conversation. The other 80 percent was on lighter topics, which became an important and necessary prelude to the deeper conversation we had later. Sometimes in these conversations we don't get to what you and I may deem "important" issues at all, and that's perfectly fine because I have learned that eventually we will discuss these weightier matters when the time is right. The groundwork needs to be laid first. Plus, I really enjoyed the first 80 percent of our discussion!

What does this have to do with work? I often observe that leaders in my network forget the 80/20 rule applies to work conversations as well. We are typically so busy that we don't feel we have the time to invest in a conversation that deviates from the business at hand. What a missed opportunity! We often fail to learn about how our colleagues are really doing, especially during difficult economic times and with the lack of civility so pervasive in our country. We may get perfunctory answers to our work questions instead of the more honest and open discussions we should be seeking. Perhaps the answer is more patience and better listening on our part. Perhaps we should meet our team members and colleagues where they are and invest in getting to know more about their interests and lives outside of work. We may need to simply ask their opinion with a sincere desire to hear their thoughts . . . and just absorb what they say without judgment. By the way, this investment in curiosity, listening, and discussing the personal side of life builds *trust*, which is an essential building block of strong relationships.

I can't think of a single business leader who would not benefit from more substantive conversations at work. If this is a challenge you face, consider the lessons of the 80/20 rule. Take time to invest in meeting people where they are and be more patient. Be intentional about scheduling one-on-one conversations with work being only a sliver of the agenda and the rest a good old-fashioned conversation filled with life, family, struggles, successes, and hopefully a little humor. Ask questions with a genuine desire to learn about the other person and be vulnerable enough to share about your life. Show sincere interest in what they are saying. Be empathetic. Be patient.

The 80/20 approach is not always perfect, but eventually you will achieve richer and more meaningful discussions with those around you at work. You will also promote better connectedness and engagement. Doesn't this payoff justify the effort?

Engage this week at work with at least one colleague in an 80/20-style conversation like the one described in this chapter. Take note of their reaction and willingness to talk openly with you. Be patient—it may take a few tries to get it right. Make this a consistent practice going forward.

CONCLUSION

Thoughtfulness is the intersection of deep reflection and broad concern for others.

ADAM GRANT

Becoming a More Thoughtful Leader was never intended to be the defining gold standard for how leaders can be the masters of thoughtfulness in their daily work. It is not a novel that tells a compelling story filled with heroes and heroines, and it is not the last book you will ever need to read about leadership. This book was simply written through my passion for reflection and thoughtfulness in a way I hope will provoke the same passion in you. It was written to be a catalyst for pursuing a deeper journey as a thoughtful leader, not the book you read at the end of the journey.

I suspect you are already a good leader at this moment in time—or you are on the road to becoming one. I intended this book and its eclectic mix of leadership topics to stimulate deeper thinking on how you can continue to learn and grow in all the areas addressed in the chapters you have just read. It is also my sincere hope that you will take what you have learned and share your newfound wisdom with those around you at work and in other areas of your life. I encourage you to take up the two investment challenges I shared in the Introduction and embrace the clarity of author Adam Grant's quote: "Thoughtfulness is the intersection of deep reflection and broad concern for others."

In the broad spectrum of leadership, *thoughtful leaders* stand out like beacons of self-awareness, empathy, compassion, and wisdom. They not only lead their troops in the daily battles of the work world, but they make sure their team members and colleagues are seen, heard, valued, and invested in. They actively practice *Ti voglio bene* ("I want your good.")

What Are Some Traits of a Thoughtful Leader?

- **They practice self-reflection and value candid feedback.** Thoughtful leaders are willing to look in the mirror, carefully consider their past actions and behaviors, and are always willing to learn and grow. They seek candid feedback from team members, peers, and other work colleagues without defensiveness and are willing to make necessary changes.

- **They are great at active listening.** They don't just wait for their turn to speak, but are sincerely interested in what you have to say. They ask great follow-up questions and follow up on what they have heard. They make it safe to be open and transparent.

- **They are empathetic and caring.** They embody *Ti voglio bene* thinking and always strive to seek their good. They can listen without judgment and seek to understand the other person's perspective, emotions, concerns, and needs.

- **They enthusiastically embrace the roles of coach, mentor, and guide.** The second of the two challenges you received in the Introduction was to invest in others. Thoughtful leaders are consistently willing, and even eager, to help those around them grow. They are both seeking to learn and grow themselves and pass along these learnings to their colleagues. They are also willing to be vulnerable and share their own struggles and failures as teachable moments.

- **They "walk the talk."** Thoughtful leaders lead by example. They are authentic and truly believe in what they are sharing with others and asking them to do. Their leadership consistently embodies the behaviors, values and pursuit of excellence they wish to see from their team members and colleagues.

It is somewhat easy to be a *thought leader*—loosely defined as being an expert at something. It is more of a challenge to be a *thoughtful leader* and care not only about your own growth, but also the growth of those you lead. Further developing the traits above and embracing the learnings from the chapters you have just read will absolutely help you on the path to being a more thoughtful leader.

I would like to share one more insight with you. As you likely gleaned from reading Chapter 10, I have a great fondness for taking long walks. Much of my writing over the years (and certainly this book) began with deep thinking that likely had its origin on a walking trail near my home or during vacations. I believe this practice has activated and enhanced my own thoughtfulness and helped me grow in countess other ways. I would like to introduce you to one of my favorite phrases: *solvitur ambulando* (Latin for "solved by walking").

The concept goes back to the ancient Greeks philosophizing

over the certainty of motion. Thousands of years ago, the philosopher Zeno posed the problem of whether or not motion was real, and his colleague Diogenes got up and walked out of the room. Offended by Diogenes' rude exit, Zeno asked what he was doing, and Diogenes responded by saying he had just proved that motion was real—"solved by walking." Centuries later, St. Augustine of Hippo coined the expression using its Latin phrasing, inferring that theological issues of the heart, soul, and mind are better "solved by walking" instead of just talking about them.

I indulge my great passion for taking long walks every day. I do it for exercise, disconnect from technology and media, clear my head, and pray. There are many other challenges for which walking is a helpful part of the solution. In our culture of overwork, burnout, and high stress, when we're over-connected and distracted from most things that are truly important in our lives, how do we tap into our creativity, deeper thinking, capacity for wonder, well-being, and ability to carefully consider how to better engage with and help our fellow humans? I have identified walking as a fundamental catalyst for my own pursuit of greater thoughtfulness, and I hope you have something equally helpful in your own life. If you are seeking ideas to jump-start greater thoughtfulness in your own life, I hope you consider the wisdom of *solvitur ambulando* as a possible answer.

I hope you enjoyed this book, and I hope it will make a positive difference in your life. I also encourage you to consider reading my 2021 book, *Essential Wisdom for Leaders of Every Generation*, and my 2022 release, *Upon Reflection: Helpful Insights and Timeless Lessons for the Busy Professional.*

CONCLUSION

Reading them all will greatly enhance the life and career journey you are on.

Thank you.

ACKNOWLEDGMENTS

I am grateful to wear a lot of important hats as a man of faith, husband, father, son, friend, business owner, executive coach, author, and community servant. After the completion of one of my books, I'm always bewildered at how it was completed with all the other priorities that occupy my attention and keep me busy. This book was no different. I have come to believe that what motivates me to write is simply a genuine desire to help my growing network thrive and grow through my humble experiences and ongoing observations about life and work. *Becoming a More Thoughtful Leader* is my latest effort to invest in leaders and aspiring leaders, and I hope you have found it helpful.

I want to first thank God for the privilege to do work I truly enjoy each day, and I pray it will be for His honor and glory, not mine. I am always grateful for my wife and sons. Their love and support that allow me to do what I do means the world to me. My father, Steve, who I often mention in my books, continues to be an inspiration for me about the right way to live and treat the people we encounter each day.

Thank you to my longtime editor Claudia Volkman for her guidance, collaboration, and expertise in shaping the final version of this book and all the other books we have collaborated on over the years. I am grateful to Karen Daniel for the book cover design and all the other covers and work we have collaborated on over the last several years. These ladies do exceptional work and have added tremendous value to the book you have just finished and all the other projects we have done together over the years.

To all my friends, clients, and collaborators who reviewed the book, offered suggestions, wrote recommendations, and simply offered encouragement, I thank you. Thank you to my clients and business colleagues who provide a school of learning, insight, and new ideas each day for me that I will never grow tired of attending. Andreas Widmer wrote a beautiful foreword for the book, but he is also the friend who taught me the priceless value of *Ti voglio bene* . . . and for this I will always be grateful.

Finally, to all the thoughtful leaders in the world who are committed to growing yourselves and helping everyone around you thrive, I thank you. You inspire me and countless others by your commitment and example. The world is a better place because of your leadership, continual focus on getting better, and the way you embrace servant leadership.

ABOUT THE AUTHOR

Randy Hain is the founder and president of Serviam Partners (ServiamPartners.com) and the co-founder of the Leadership Foundry (MyLeadershipFoundry.com). With a successful thirty-plus-year career in senior leadership roles, corporate talent, and executive search, he is a sought-after executive coach for senior leaders at some of the best-known companies in the United States who are seeking expert guidance on identifying and overcoming obstacles to their success or developing new leadership skills. He is also an expert at onboarding and cultural assimilation for senior leaders as well as helping senior leadership teams improve trust, clarity, collaboration, and candid communication. Randy also offers consulting and coaching for companies, teams, and individual business leaders looking to develop more authentic and effective business relationships both inside and outside their organizations. His deep expertise in business relationships is a true area of differentiation for him and Serviam Partners.

He is an active community leader and serves on the boards of organizations he cares about most. He is a longtime partner of the SEC (Southeastern Conference) Career Tour and presents on career readiness topics to the student-athletes and other leadership topics to leaders from the various SEC schools. As a member of the advisory board for the Brock School of Business at Samford University, Randy frequently presents on relevant business and career topics to the Samford students. He is passionate about promoting autism awareness and advocating for adults with autism in the workplace. He is also an active member of St. Peter Chanel Catholic Church. Randy has earned a reputation as a creative business partner and generous thought leader through his books, articles, and speaking engagements.

Randy is the award-winning author of ten other books, including *Being Fully Present, Upon Reflection: Helpful Insights and Timeless Lessons for the Busy Professional, Essential Wisdom for Leaders of Every Generation, Something More: The Professional's Pursuit of a Meaningful Life, LANDED! Proven Job Search Strategies for Today's Professional*, and *Special Children, Blessed Fathers: Encouragement for Fathers of Children with Special Needs*, all available on Amazon.

More books by Randy Hain

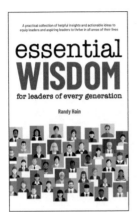

Essential Wisdom for Leaders of Every Generation

A practical collection of helpful insights and actionable ideas to equip leaders and aspiring leaders to thrive in all areas of their lives.

Essential Wisdom for Leaders of Every Generation, Randy Hain's eighth book, offers today's leaders and aspiring leaders a practical collection of helpful advice and actionable ideas drawn from his thirty-plus years of senior leadership, coaching, and consulting experience to successfully navigate all areas of their lives.

Essential Wisdom is a must-have guidebook filled with insights, ideas, and best practices that all professionals should think about and do well in order to be more effective in their roles. Leaders and aspiring leaders of every age and any stage of their career journey will find practical nuggets of wisdom they can use to accelerate their success.

Upon Reflection

Helpful insights and timeless lessons for the busy professional.

Randy Hain's ninth book offers timeless lessons and practical ideas on a myriad of topics drawn from his 30+ years of senior leadership, executive coaching, and consulting experience to help fuel the career success and personal growth of busy professionals from every generation.

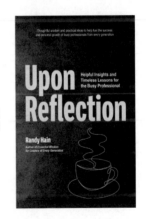

Written through the author's own practice of intentional reflection, Upon Reflection is a thoughtful book that will benefit everyone. Experienced professionals will gain helpful new perspectives and be reminded of what they hopefully know and believe but sometimes forget to practice. Younger professionals discover valuable insights into the timeless values, virtues, and best practices that make for a richer life and a successful career. All readers will find great value in the various relevant topics and encouragement the book offers to slow down, savor the moments, and be more reflective.

All books available on Amazon

Made in the USA
Columbia, SC
24 September 2024